The Fortifications of Butrint

Gjerak Karaiskaj

English edition of *Butrinti dhe fortifikimet e tij* (Tirana 1984)
edited by Andrew Crowson

BUTRINT FOUNDATION
2009

Acknowledgements

The Butrint Foundation and The International Centre for Albanian Archaeology are grateful to The Packard Humanities Institute for the generous grants that made the publication of this book possible. The editing of the revised text was assisted by Alison Ferrary and Rupert Smith. Karaiskaj's original text was translated into English by Brikena Shkodra, and amendments made by Karaiskaj in 2006 were translated by Jonida Martini. The illustrations in this edition are either redrawn from the originals or are modern colour images taken to replicate the black and white photographs contained in the original book. When it was not possible to identify, locate or access features illustrated in the original photographs, these have either been omitted or replaced with comparable images. The photographs and maps are by Richard Andrews, Brian Donovan, Giovanni Lattanzi, Martin Smith and members of the Butrint Foundation and ICAA teams: Andrew Crowson, Amy Culwick, Oliver J. Gilkes, Valbona Hysa, Klodiana Kondo, Matthew Logue, Nevila Molla, Rene Rice and Rupert Smith. We are grateful for the permission to reproduce images granted by the Instituti i Arkeologjisë (Tirana). Unless otherwise stated all illustrations are copyright of the Butrint Foundation.

Contents

Preface to the English edition 7

Foreword 11

Introduction 13

Previous studies 17

The 6th–2nd centuries BC: Archaic to Hellenistic structures 25
Historical context; The defensive walls; Styles and techniques of construction; The gates; The Dema Wall; Dating the walls

The 1st century BC–6th century AD: Roman and late antique structures 51
Historical context; The Roman defensive walls; Construction techniques; The late antique fortifications

The 7th–15th centuries AD: medieval structures 65
Historical context; The outer fortified wall circuit; The wall linking the acropolis and the lakeshore; The fortifications of the acropolis; The wall between the acropolis and the Lake Gate; The Acropolis Castle; Construction techniques

The late 13th–19th centuries: Venetian and Ottoman structures 91
Historical context; The Triangular Fortress; The Venetian Tower and the Watchtower; Dating the channel-side fortifications; Ali Pasha's Castle

Conclusions 121

References 125

Colour plates 131

Preface to the English edition

Gjerak Karaiskaj's work on the fortifications of Butrint is one of the single most significant archaeological discourses produced during the communist era in Albania (1945-91) and the most important for Butrint. Published in Albanian in 1984 not only did it become the point of reference for all future studies of the ancient city's military architecture, but it encapsulated perfectly the political historical paradigm within which Karaiskaj was obliged to operate. Based on a foundation of technical description within a historical storyline underpinned by assertions of ethnicity and origin, *The Fortifications of Butrint* weaves the Socialists' reasoned tale through the contention of past scholars.

Karaiskaj published a prodigious number of archaeological articles throughout the 1970s and 1980s. Working all around the country, and alongside contemporary luminaries in the field such as Apollon Baçe, Neritan Ceka and Aleksandër Meksi, Karaiskaj became pre-eminent in the study of Albania's fortifications. Against an academic backdrop of a quest for everything Illyrian, his interests included the country's prehistoric fortified settlements, its early Roman fortifications, and developed a particular emphasis on late antique fortified towns and medieval castles and towers. In these studies, politically important themes of the origin and development of urban areas were constant if inherent concerns. Then, in 1981, a decade of research and fieldwork yielded Karaiskaj's most important work, the monograph *5000 Years of Fortifications in Albania*.

For his study of the fortification of Butrint Karaiskaj took the work of Italian archaeologist Luigi Maria Ugolini as his baseline. Though Ugolini's work was already some 50 years old and conducted under a different political imperative, it was still the principal authoritative voice on Butrint's fortifications. Reproducing some of the earlier plans, Karaiskaj set out to reframe the social, economic and political history of the city told through its walls, towers, gateways and castles. With no opportunity for fresh excavations, with largely out-dated reference material and supported by the results of only small-scale archaeological work by his contemporaries, Karaiskaj achieved many of his typological interpretations and much of his topographic phasing through comparative and stylistic judgement alone.

Whilst one of *The Fortifications of Butrint*'s central tenets – that of continuity of habitation at Butrint – may merit some reconsideration, the theory represented one of the communist government's many 'truth without proof' doctrines, namely a Marxist-inspired view of an ethnically, culturally and socially unbroken succession from the ancient Illyrians down to modern Albanians. The assertion of a distinct national identity was fundamental to Albania's increasingly self-imposed isolation and self-reliance at this time and the country's archaeologists were in turn a pivotal tool in constructing and maintaining a predetermined historical model. Consequently, socialist Albania pursued a vigorous campaign of publishing national historical and archaeological studies

In May 2004, the Butrint Foundation, entering its 10th year of working at Butrint, set up a small project to re-evaluate its own and earlier studies on the city's medieval and Venetian castles and defences. Gjerak Karaiskaj, then Director of the Albanian Institute of Monuments, joined as a partner and led an excavation of a late antique tower. As part of this project, an interview and tour around Butrint was conducted with him. During this fascinating encounter the physical and academic conditions under which Karaiskaj performed his original surveys and assessments were brought into sharp focus. Granted no more than a week to complete his fieldwork and escorted by a military guard to ensure he did not abscond across the nearby border with Greece, his accomplishment appears all the more remarkable. The pace at which the data for the book was assembled may account for the occasional repetition in the narrative and the complexity of the task in hand excuses the rare examples of evident ambiguity.

Karaiskaj's original 1984 book was published with a print run of only 3,000 copies, though did contain a substantial summary in German. Following the 2004 meeting with the author, however, the Butrint Foundation resolved to translate and re-publish *The Fortifications of Butrint* in an English language edition. Whilst becoming a part of the Foundation's aim to re-assess, interpret and publish archive materials pertaining to Butrint, the English edition opens up this influential book and its historical context to a broader, and more critical, international readership.

Post-communism, the debate over continuity of occupation and persistence of urban or otherwise populations in towns continues to exercise Albanian archaeologists. The perfunctory Western, anti-continuity, anti-Illyrian ancestry viewpoint is now softening to concede a degree of durability. Archaeological survey and excavation undertaken in Butrint during the intervening 24 years between the original publication and this translated edition have, however, indubitably shed fresh light on some of the more contentious aspects of Karaiskaj's typological phasing and interpretation of the fortification sequences. For example, it now appears most likely that the first true fortification walls in Butrint belong to the time of Pyrrhus of Epirus in the early 3rd century BC; the late Roman waterfront walls and probably the western *proteichisma* can be dated to the final quarter of the 5th century AD; and the complex sequencing of the Byzantine,

Despotic and Venetian period defences and urban organisation is gradually being unravelled and demystified (a select list of recent publications is given below). This notwithstanding, *The Fortifications of Butrint* retains much to be admired and remains an important piece of period scholarship. At a time when Butrint is becoming one of the primary sites for heritage tourism in the eastern central Mediterranean, it is right that Karaiskaj's work should be reinvigorated and re-presented to a new and inquisitive audience.

Andrew Crowson
2008

Recent Butrint Foundation publications:

Bowden, W. (2003) *Epirus Vetus: The Archaeology of a Late Antique Province.* London, Duckworth.

Crowson, A. (2007) *Butrinti Venecian / Venetian Butrint.* London/Tirana, Butrint Foundation.

Gilkes, O.J. (2003) (ed.) *The Theatre at Butrint. Luigi Maria Ugolini's Excavations at Butrint 1928-1932* (*Albania antica* IV). London, British School at Athens.

Hansen, I.L. and Hodges, R. (2007) (eds), *Roman Butrint. An Assessment.* Oxford, Oxbow.

Hansen, I.L., Gilkes, O.J. and Crowson, A. (2005) *Kalivo and Çuka e Aitoit, Albania. Interim Report on Surveys and Excavations 1928-2004.* www.butrintfoundation.co.uk.

Hodges, R. (2008) *Shkëlqimi dhe rënia e Butrintit bizantin / The Rise and Fall of Byzantine Butrint.* London/Tirana, Butrint Foundation.

Hodges, R., Bowden, W. and Lako, K. (2004) (eds.) *Byzantine Butrint: Excavations and Survey 1994-1999.* Oxford, Oxbow.

Mitchell, J. (2008) *Pagëzimorja e Butrintit dhe mozaikët e saj / The Butrint Baptistery and its Mosaics.* London/Tirana, Butrint Foundation.

Foreword

The principal objective of this book is a study of the defensive constructions of Butrint throughout all periods of its history. The major historical events of the city and its surroundings, as well as the socio-economic and political history of the region provide the context for this analysis. A second objective is to ascertain the accuracy of previous plans. Study of the defensive structures, which have such an important place in the architecture of the city, will serve to complete the historical picture and contribute to the investigation of the continuity of this centre of occupation from prehistory to the late medieval period.

Through the analysis of different building phases and techniques, this survey further aims to provide a point of reference for conservation and restoration projects, and to contribute to the preservation of the archaeological monuments.

The study of the defensive structures at Butrint started with the Triangular Fortress and the fortifications along the banks of the Vivari Channel, which were restored in 1975. Several restoration and study expeditions took place in 1976 and 1977. These projects enabled the fieldwork needed for a general analysis of Butrint's fortifications and the opportunity to understand their individual elements. The study of the monuments is based on the existing remains of the circuit walls and the other defensive constructions in Butrint. In some cases data from archaeological excavations, published or commented on by other authors, have been used.

The methods employed here comprise an analytical study of the monuments themselves, through determining their various structural phases by examining construction techniques and identifying architectural elements. Dating is based on comparison with other structures both within and without Albania, and on consideration of the historical circumstances that might have promoted or deferred the construction of the city's defences. Establishing a construction typology for the medieval period was particularly difficult due to the paucity of research on this topic in neighbouring countries. Hence the typological study is often limited to construction techniques alone. Future studies will require more survey and archaeological excavations, as well as greater research into these types of structures in the territories of the Byzantine Empire in surrounding countries.

New data, derived from excavation of a rectangular tower in the city's western defences in 2004, has added important information to the original study. Conducted by Solinda Kamani and myself, the cleaning and superficial excavations to trace the double western wall led to the discovery of a medieval *proteichisma*, which will be the subject of a focused study in the future.[1]

The 1977 study of the defensive walls of Butrint, which was the subject of the dissertation for my degree (known then as a 'Science Candidate', now called a 'Doctorate'), was made possible by the extraordinary care of the archaeologist Dhimitër Çondi, under whose guidance workmen cleared vegetation from areas close to the fortification walls to facilitate observation. Since then no such comprehensive clearance has been made and many parts of the fortifications have remained inaccessible.

A peculiar thing happened on this expedition that is scarcely believable nowadays. A strange, foreboding feeling made me finish collecting the most important data needed within a week. Indeed, no sooner had I finished, than I was forbidden by the Institute of Monuments, in collaboration with the Secret Police, to return to Butrint. The area was at that time considered a border zone from where it might be possible to escape Albania, and hence a place of particular state concern. The restoration work on the Triangular Fortress was also abandoned and I was replaced at the Institute of Monuments with another trusted specialist. However, thanks to my premonition, I collected most of the data necessary and the book was subsequently published in 1984.

Gjerak Karaiskaj
2006

---

[1] Editor's note: study and excavation of the towers in the Western Defences has continued under the direction of S. Kamani between 2006-8, revealing an extraordinary phase of Byzantine period occupation; see Hodges 2008.

Introduction

Butrint lies on the southeast tip of the Ksamil peninsula, a narrow neck of land located a few kilometres south of the town of Saranda (Plates 1 and 3). The Ionian Sea washes the western shores of the peninsula, whilst to its east is Lake Butrint (known in ancient times by the name *Pelodes*). To the south, at Butrint, the peninsula is severed by the waters of the Vivari Channel that connect the lake to the sea. Surrounded by water on three sides, the ruins of the ancient city are located on a low limestone hill with steep rock outcrops on its south face. The walled city is connected to the peninsula only by a narrow isthmus on its west side (Plate 4).

The solid geology at Butrint consists, for the most part, of limestone formations. The rocky acropolis hill stands to a relative height of around 45 m at its east end, and measures at its widest points c. 270 m northeast-southwest x 90 m northwest-southeast. The rocky outcrops of the hill enabled some quarrying for early buildings, which may have steepened the southern acropolis face and increased its defensive potential. The city's watery perimeter added to the protective value of the site and provided rich fishing and safe anchorage for trade. An expansive panorama can be viewed from the acropolis, obscured only to the north by the higher hills of the peninsula: to the west, the island and Straits of Corfu are in plain sight; to the south, the valley plains of Vrina and Xarra (ancient Cestrina), and the coastal hill fringe of Cape Styllo; and to the east, the far shores of Lake Butrint and the high prominence of the hill range of Mt Mile.

This favourable natural situation coupled with a regionally significant location gave rise to habitation at Butrint in prehistoric times that later flourished in an expanding city from at least the early 3rd century BC. Although Butrint maintained its strategic importance through to the Napoleonic Wars, it began to decline as a town centre from the high medieval period due to environmental change: fluctuating water levels inundated lower parts of the city and reduced much of the surrounding fertile land to marsh. The denizens abandoned the city and plains to find fresh shelter in the hills.

Other fortified settlements and fortresses around Butrint were both important and numerous, especially so in prehistoric and pre-Roman times (Plate 3). To the north, the Dema Wall, constructed across the neck of the Ksamil peninsula, was intrinsically linked to the protection of Butrint. Built by the Prasaebian tribe before the close of the 3rd century BC, it was refortified during late antiquity.

The fortification on the summit of Çuka e Ajtoit marks the southern extent of the region's fortified sites (Plate 3). Situated to the south of the Pavllas River, on a high conical hill, a settlement covers an area of *c.* 5 ha within encircling walls 1,400 m long. The fortification is divided into two parts: the top of the hill is surrounded by a wall without towers, though their function is achieved by numerous angles in the wall line, and the west flank is guarded by an additional walled terrace. In the latter section, the fortification wall, besides its angles and defensive bastions, also includes towers that largely served to protect the otherwise vulnerable entrances. The enceinte has six entrances, located principally in the southern extent. The defensive walls have a width of 3.50 m, and incorporate a mixture of different styles and forms: polygonal; coursed trapezoidal; and isodomic trapezoidal. These styles are intermingled and date from a single period of construction.

East of Butrint, on the shore of Lake Butrint, lies the fortified settlement of Kalivo (Plate 3). Defensive walls surround the upper part of a saddle-backed hill, surrounded by the waters of Lake Butrint on all sides bar the southeast. To the north and west the hill drops steeply to the lake, and for this reason the hill remained undefended on this approach. Elsewhere fortification walls survive up to 4 m in height and width. The stones are typically large, un-worked and ill-fitting in comparison to the early walls at Butrint. Three entrances, protected by internal passageways and equipped with steps lead to the interior.

At the northeast corner of Lake Butrint, the fortification of Karalibej occupies a hilltop that dominates the passage along the east side of the lake towards the Pavllas valley (Plate 3). The style and construction technique of its walls are akin to those of the 6th–2nd-century BC building phase in Butrint.

In the southeast of the Mile mountain range, a fortified prehistoric enclosure with a wall perimeter of 170 m commanded the Bogazi gorge, the eastern gateway to the Pavllas valley. Nearby stands an isolated pre-Roman tower known as the Tower of Vagalat (Plate 3). The rectangular tower survives to the height of the first floor and measures 9.50 x 6.50 m. It is approached from above by a broad stepped ramp that was constructed as a double wall, tied together with perpendicular blocks, and measuring 3.50 m wide. The tower and ramp were built from rectangular stone blocks (robbed and re-worked from the prehistoric enclosure) in even courses 0.35 to 0.45 m high.

The fortified villa of Malathrea, constructed in the same technique as the Tower of Vagalat, is situated low on the east valley side between Butrint and Çuka e Ajtoit. It is rectangular in plan with corner towers and numerous inter-connected internal rooms. A number of archaeological artefacts dating from the centuries around the time of Christ (Ceka 1976: 38) have been found on the site.

Also worth mention is a tower uncovered in the modern village of Çuka at the head of Lake Butrint. It is constructed of neatly carved dry stone blocks. Associated archaeological material dates its construction to the 2nd or 1st century BC. A similar construction can be seen at Metoq near Saranda.

Situated immediately east of Saranda, on a high hill overlooking the town, is the medieval castle of Lëkurës. A typical garrison fortification, it is square-shaped in plan, with two round corner towers. Constructed around the 17th-18th centuries it overlooked Saranda harbour and the eastern approach to the town through Gjashta along the road that connected Butrint to the Delvina basin during the period when Butrint was under Venetian dominion.

Though constructed and occupied in different periods, all of the fortified centres detailed briefly above, including other fortifications such as the Castle of Qenurio, may be linked, in one way or another, to the ancient city of Butrint (Plate 3).

Previous studies

The earliest antiquarian to visit Butrint was the Humanist scholar and traveller Cyriacus of Ancona who visited the ancient city as part of a journey to Greece in 1435. Enthused by what he found, Cyriacus sketched some of the ruined buildings, recorded sculptural fragments and copied two inscriptions. In the early part of the 19th century, Butrint was seen by diplomats from Britain and Austria, namely Colonel William Martin Leake (Leake 1835: 101) and Anton Graf von Prokesch-Osten, who both wrote topographic accounts of the ruins. Some time later, the French travel-writer Emile Isambert also wrote a short description of the city (Isambert 1873: 835).

Subsequent to this early interest in the monuments of Butrint, the first systematic study, recording and excavation of the city was begun in 1926 by an Italian archaeological mission led by Luigi Maria Ugolini, who directed the work until his death in 1936. The Italian mission comprised a diverse group of scholars including architects, painters, conservators, numismatists and specialists in the study of Venetian fortifications. Ugolini's research was published in numerous articles and summarised in the monographs *Butrinto, il mito d'Enea. Gli scavi* (1937) and *Albania Antica III, l'acropoli di Butrinto* (1942). Ugolini's assessment of the city's multi-period fortifications may be summarised as follows: in the pre-Roman period Butrint was protected by three successive lines of walls positioned at different elevations on the acropolis hillside. The wall surrounding the flat area at the top of the hill, named the 'pelasgic' type, was determined to be the earliest. The second wall, situated halfway up the southern and western faces of the hill and along the northern lake shore, was classified by Ugolini as 'with polygonal blocks' and was considered to represent improvement and extension of the earlier, more rudimentary walls. The third wall line, at the base of the hill on the south side, was constructed to allow expansion of the growing town that had become constricted inside the earlier walls.

Ugolini proposed that the latest of the three wall circuits, which is also the best preserved, can be dated to the 5th–4th centuries BC. This date was determined on stylistic criteria, based on a characteristic construction technique of using huge, regular rectangular blocks. The same style was also observed in ruined sections of earlier walls (Ugolini 1937: 116-17). Ugolini attempted a more detailed classification of Butrint's city walls in *L'Acropoli di Butrinto*, to achieve a more complete chronology of the different phases of construction. In total, he distinguished five distinct stylistic phases based on the cutting and setting of the masonry, from the earliest to the latest: 'pelasgic'; polygonal; stones with six to eight sides with blocks taller than they are wide; large rectangular blocks; and small rectangular blocks set in regular courses. Refining his chronology further, Ugolini dated the third phase, which includes the masonry of the Lake Gate, to the late 5th to early 4th century BC, the fourth phase to the mid 4th century BC and the fifth phase to *c.* the 3rd century BC (Ugolini 1942: 44).

The fortification walls of the Roman and later periods are bonded with mortar and frequently erected over ancient buildings. Wherever Ugolini encountered these walls he considered them to be 'medieval'. Aside from being unable to distinguish the different phases of later construction, he concluded that they offer little useful chronological information; rather they simply show the numerous reconstructions in the medieval period (Ugolini 1937: 95). Ugolini comments, 'Without doubt, many sections of the fortifications belong to the Venetian period, while the earliest ones can be attributed to the period from the end of the Roman Empire to the first [barbarian] incursions' (Ugolini 1937: 170). Remarking on the deficiency of the fortifications in the early part of the Roman period he notes, 'the fact that the Romans, absolute rulers of Butrint and of the whole region, could have restored the surrounding walls [but did not] is very surprising, but true. In addition we have to consider that … maybe the majority [of restorations] have been made in Late Antiquity, which can be explained by barbarian invasions.'

Although hesitant to study the medieval fortifications in detail, Ugolini considered many of Butrint's later fortifications, such as the Acropolis Castle, the so-called Venetian Tower on the north bank of the Vivari Channel, the Triangular Fortress on the opposite bank and Ali Pasha's Castle at the mouth of the channel, to date from the Venetian period. However, in an illustrated chronological table of different wall building techniques, Ugolini precisely defines several Roman techniques, yet cannot find them in the fortification walls of Butrint. Furthermore, he includes a late antique style with tile courses in this group, while some medieval techniques, similar to *cloisonné* masonry, are classified as late antique (Ugolini 1937).

In 1932 the British classical scholar N.G.L. Hammond visited the ruined city and discussed the excavations with Ugolini. Hammond was interested in the ancient history of Butrint and particularly its fortifications. The notes he made during this visit were later published in *Epirus* (1967). Hammond rightly disputed the second phase wall circuit as defined by Ugolini, though he was mistaken in his contention that the wall above the Theatre was a retaining or terrace wall (Hammond 1967: 109). Furthermore, he proposed a third (late) type of polygonal masonry. Hammond also differed from the Italians in his stylistic interpretations of the walls. He asserted that a variety of ashlar style construction was the most common, within which block size, coursing and use of rabbeting might distinguish separate constructional events. Discussing the phase of ashlar blocks, which constitutes the principal defensive wall circuit and the most complete phase of Butrint's early fortifications, Hammond described the 'variety of ashlar style in which rabbeting is liberally used' and where vertical joints are not always perpendicular. He remarked, 'this rabbeting tends to upset the regularity of the horizontal courses' (Hammond 1967: 100). Hammond concluded that the use of different sized ashlars did not indicate chronological differences, but left room to admit the possibility that if chronologically distinct, they represented sub-divisions of a single period in which rabbeting was employed. Hammond thus determined that the five building periods distinguished by Ugolini could be reduced to three, and that the ashlar built walls represent the first complete enceinte.

After the death of Ugolini, the excavations at Butrint were continued by his colleague Pirro Marconi. He perished in an air accident in 1938, reportedly with much of the excavation archive. Marconi's excavations were notable for exploring the ancient fortifications on the south side of the acropolis and, most importantly, for the discovery of a 'new' gate in the lower circuit protected by two flanking towers (giving rise to the name of the 'Tower Gate'). Today the only documentation to survive from the excavation of this gate is a reconstruction sketch held in the archive of the Institute of Archaeology in Tirana. In turn, the work of Marconi was taken over by Domenico Mustilli, who continued to direct excavations at Butrint until 1941 (Mustilli 1941). He dated the Tower Gate to the 3rd century BC, proposing a context of Epirote defence against perceived threats from the Illyrian state.

Mustilli postulated that Butrint was founded by Greek colonists around the end of the 7th century BC. He considered that the walls with irregular blocks, comprising the earliest enceinte, might have pre-dated the arrival of the colonists and that the extension of the city's defensive system with the ashlar walls of the

Lake Gate type dated to the end of the 5th century BC. Like his forerunners, Mustilli did not distinguish the Roman fortifications from the medieval walls. With some assurance he stated that, with the *Pax Romana* (Roman Peace), the character of the city changed; the walls were no longer required for protection and were subsequently incorporated in both private and public structures, while the settlement expanded over the open flat ground to the side of the Vivari Channel (Mustilli 1940: 6). With only minor revision, Mustilli supported Ugolini's interpretation of the medieval fortifications, attributing the refortification of the acropolis, the construction of the Acropolis Castle itself and the Triangular Fortress on the south bank of the channel to the Venetians (Mustilli 1940: 11). Pellegrino Claudio Sestieri was the final Italian scholar of that generation to consider Butrint (Drini 1943; Sestieri 1942; 1943; 1959). However, he did not arrive at any new interpretations from those of his predecessors, being content with the sum of the conclusions achieved at the time of the Italian archaeological mission.

It is apposite to point out that the whole strategy of the Italian mission was incorporated into the chauvinistic political aims of Rome towards Albania. Its aim was to praise highly Albania's Roman and Venetian material cultural heritage in order to present past Italian invasions of the country as a positive phenomenon and to prepare the ground for a fresh invasion. Explaining the origins of Butrint through the legend of Aeneas was to argue that the two coasts of the Adriatic had shared a common destiny from antiquity. These goals were expressed quite openly and without shame after the occupation of Albania by Fascist Italy in 1939, when an Italian newspaper wrote 'The voice of the hero (Aeneas) that reaches us, still alive after so many centuries and thousands of years, gains strength and higher value today, when the myth is accomplished and Albania is united with Italy.'

After the Second World War investigations continued at Butrint as part of a programme of archaeological excavations and research across the country and covering different periods of the rich history of Albania. Initially, excavations directed by Dhimosten Budina were focused on the necropolis of Butrint outside the encircling walls where ten graves dating from the Hellenistic period to the 1st century AD were recorded (Budina 1959: 246-56). One of the monuments of Butrint not examined by the Italians, due to marsh and dense vegetation on the Vrina Plain, was the city's aqueduct, this Budina traced and studied (Budina 1967:145).

Inscriptions carved on the western *parodos* wall of the Theatre were copied by the epigrapher Luigi Morricone before the Second World War but were not published until a short review of their content was provided by Margherita

Guarducci in the 1950s (Guarducci 1953). Budina with Koço Bozhori sought to give an integrated description of these inscriptions, to serve for other specialists to interpret them (Bozhori and Budina 1966). The authors did not fully achieve their objectives, as a critical article and short description of the inscriptions by Hasan Ceka pointed out (Ceka 1967). He emphasized the particular features of Prasaebian institutions distinct from those of the Greek colonies and *poleis* and touched on the formation of the *koinon* of the Prasaebians, which he related to events after 168 BC and, in particular, after the death of Charops II. The emergence of this tribe is seen as a result of the Roman policy of 'divide and rule' that set them against the powerful Chaonian tribe. In the 1970s a complete interpretation of the inscriptions, which are an important historical source for the social and political organization of Butrint, the ethnic history of its inhabitants, as well as for the solution of a number of historical issues of the area around Butrint, was provided by the French epigrapher Pierre Cabanes (Cabanes 1974; 1976). Finally, the inscriptions have been used to determine a date of 230 BC for the construction of the Theatre (Guarducci 1953).

One of the main entrances into the city, the Lion Gate, was studied by Koço Zheku who distinguished two phases of construction during restoration work on the gate (Zheku 1971). Zheku determined that the dimensions of the original entrance became much reduced in both height and width through the application of new facing stones and the lowering of the lion relief architrave. Working from Ugolini's estimates, Zheku placed the original construction of the gate in the 4th century BC and its reduction some time during late antiquity (Zheku 1971: 79). Moreover, he argued that the Lion Gate was not in use during the Middle Ages as a square tower with a roof was built over it as Ugolini had proposed. In 1975 restoration works were carried out on the Tower Gate by Guri Pani (Pani 1976). During the clearance of vegetation a second entrance was discovered in the wall to the west of the square (western) tower. In his reconstruction drawing of the entrance complex, Pani, unlike Marconi before him, correctly included a row of windows on the first floor of each tower as well as the second entrance adjacent to the square tower. Pani believed that the Tower Gate was constructed in the early 3rd century BC, at a time when Butrint was flourishing (Pani 1976: 42).

A project tracing the line of the city wall to the west of the Tower Gate was concluded by Kosta Lako in 1976. Lako's results concurred with those of Ugolini and Mustilli, in that after Butrint had been granted Roman colonial status, the original purpose of the ancient wall was lost and thereafter it had been amalgamated into new structures (Lako 1977-78). The wall was followed westwards for 45 m from the Tower Gate, but because of high water levels excavation did not reach the contemporary ground surface. Upper levels contained material of the 10th to 13th centuries AD. Beneath these, deposits dating from the 5th to 6th centuries were encountered. The earliest strata dated to the 2nd to 4th centuries. The most intensive period of occupation in this area occurred in the 4th century AD. Deposits of this date produced 80% of the coin assemblage from this site alongside large quantities of amphorae and cooking wares. Lako interpreted rooms on the inside of the wall as shops, and ascribed a date of late 4th to early 3rd century BC for the wall itself. In support of this date he stated 'Although the excavation did not reach ground level, the construction technique, the shape of the blocks, the similarity to walls elsewhere in Butrint (especially the similarities with the Tower Gate) and other Epirote fortifications, indicate that the wall must have been built in the late 4th to early 3rd century BC' (Lako 1977-78: 295).

The most comprehensive study of the ancient fortifications of Butrint was carried out by Neritan Ceka, who adopted a critical approach to the previous studies made by Ugolini and Hammond (Ceka 1976). Whilst joining Hammond's rejection of Ugolini's second phase enceinte, Ceka disputed the Englishman's contention that the wall on the south side of the acropolis was a retaining wall. Instead, Ceka linked the walls above the Theatre with a separate stretch of wall close to the Tower Gate and with the wall that continues east from the Tower Gate. Together with the walls of Lake Gate type, which delimit the north and west sides of the city, Ceka proposed that this line constituted the third phase of fortification at Butrint (Butrint III), which he dated to around the mid 4th century BC. Preceding this phase, Ceka postulated two phases of wall construction following the contours at the top of the acropolis hill. These he dated to the 7th to 6th century BC and to before the 4th century BC. In the final construction phase (Butrint IV), Ceka included the Tower Gate and the wall running to its west; a wall traversing the eastern slope of the acropolis to the Lake Gate; a section of wall on the southwest side of the acropolis (cf. Plate 5 K-L); as well as the south side of the Lion Gate. He suggested that in this stage the north wall of the acropolis was demolished and that the city was divided into two parts: the upper city and the lower city.

Based on stylistic interpretations of wall construction, Ceka classified the ancient fortifications at Butrint thus:

1. Simple walls with unworked stones (Butrint I)
2. Trapezoidal-polygonal walls with flat faced stones (Butrint II)
3. Trapezoidal walls with unworked stones in uneven courses (Butrint III)
4. Trapezoidal-isodomic walls (Butrint IV)

He dated the wall in front of the Theatre within the final phase, Butrint IV, to around the end of the 3rd century BC, corresponding to the earliest inscriptions in the Theatre.

Excavations to expose the city wall west of the Tower Gate continued under Budina in 1976-77, and a rectangular tower built with reused materials was discovered (the so-called Tower of Inscriptions). The inscriptions found on the stone blocks making up the tower were subsequently studied by Faik Drini revealing significant historical data on Butrint's position as the centre of the Prasaebian tribe in the mid 2nd century BC. One of the main conclusions drawn from study of the inscriptions was the existence of an independent Prasaebian state from the middle of the 2nd century BC. The Roman bath buildings in Butrint have been studied by Apollon Baçe whilst some of the palaeochristian and Byzantine monuments in the city have been examined by Aleksandër Meksi and Hasan Nallbani (Baçe 1980; Meksi 1976; Nallbani 1979).

The dating of the ancient and Byzantine fortifications has been the subject for numerous different authors and articles on Butrint. Selim Islami, for instance, includes the walls of Butrint III (Lake Gate) with the polygonal constructions and dates them to within the late 6th century to the final quarter of the 4th century BC, whereas Baçe places these walls in the 5th century BC (Islami 1975; Baçe 1979). Frano Prendi assigns the construction of the polygonal wall above the Theatre to a separate phase and attributes its construction to incoming Greek colonists who built the walls in the late 6th to early 5th century BC. According to Prendi, in the 5th century BC another enceinte of rectangular blocks was built in Butrint that encompassed the entire perimeter of the acropolis hill. He identifies some repairs made with smaller blocks in the early 3rd century BC and dates the Tower Gate to the late 4th to early 3rd century BC (Prendi 1959: 19). Prendi also considers that the Triangular Fortress, on the south bank of the Vivari Channel, was built by Ali Pasha of Tepelena.

The city's medieval fortifications are one of the most characteristic features of modern day Butrint, but have so far remained insufficiently explored. Sporadic and controversial assessments expressed by other authors to date are contradictory, inaccurate and lend nothing but confusion to establishing the true chronology of these structures.

The 6th–2nd centuries BC: Archaic to Hellenistic structures

HISTORICAL CONTEXT

The principal tribes of Epirus were the Molossians, the Thesprotians and the Chaonians. Butrint fell within the territory of the Chaonians, who, until the end of the 5th century BC, were the most formidable tribe in Epirus. According to Strabo (*Geography* 7.5), the Chaonians' domain extended as far as the Acroceraunian mountains in the north with Phoenice, which controlled the Delvina Basin, as their capital. Butrint and its surrounding area, however, were more closely connected to the sea than to the inland territories of Chaonia such as the Drino and Delvina valleys. This aspect promoted a degree of self-government in the area that later, during the period of Roman invasion, emerged with its own state organisation under the Prasaebian tribe.

Butrint is described as a town for the first time by Hecataeus of Miletus at the end of the 6th century/beginning of the 5th century BC (Muller 1841: 5). However, Pseudo-Scylax, who lived in the middle of the 4th century BC, records that the people of the Epirote tribes lived in villages. He only records the existence of two towns on the coast of Epirus: Oricum and Ambracia. Bearing in mind, though, that Pseudo-Scylax used sources earlier than Hecataeus (namely Scylax of Carianda, who was writing around the end of the 6th century BC), we cannot rule out Butrint's status as a town in the middle of the 4th century BC on this claim alone. Nevertheless, the mention of Oricum and Ambracia on the Epirote coast, but not of Butrint shows that the latter had not emerged as a town before the end of the 6th century BC. By 'town' in this period we should think of a fortified centre with administrative, economic and political functions, distinct from the scattered and unprotected villages of the age. The 'town' was a centre for trade, an attribution testified today by the presence of contemporary imported ceramics in excavations. Other prehistoric fortifications in a given area may have functioned as places of refuge in this period, where villagers could secure themselves against outside threats. The existence of unprotected or open villages has been identified in the vicinity of Butrint on the Ksamil peninsula (Çondi 1981: 12-15).

The earliest archaeological evidence to demonstrate the existence of an inhabited centre of some importance in Butrint is the ceramic artefacts discovered on the acropolis in 1938, among which Corinthian wares (dated to *c.* 6th century BC) were prevalent. Subsequent excavations on the acropolis by Katerina Hadzis in the early 1990s placed the earliest habitation of the site in the late 8th century BC. However, no architectural evidence has yet been found, with the exception of the first phase of the acropolis wall built with un-worked stones, that can be associated with this period. In later excavations Hadzis discovered local ceramics dating from the end of the 8th century–beginning of the 7th century BC as well as imported wares from Corinth and Corfu dated to the second half of the 7th century BC.

The British historian Nicholas Hammond thought that Scylax's (28) omission of Butrint marked the city out as being independent, whilst his French counterpart Pierre Cabanes believes that Butrint may have been under Corfu at that time, rather than under the Chaonians (Hammond 1967: 514; Cabanes 1976: 116). After this time, Butrint was more certainly included in the Chaonian community, but it seems to have preserved a degree of autonomy within this group. Unlike the Molossians, who were ruled by strong royal authority, from the end of the 5th century BC and during the 4th century BC the Chaonians were governed by two men who were chosen annually from among the ranks of the high aristocracy. Despite the successes of Alexander the Molossian (345-331 BC) in extending the territorial borders of the Molossian League, the Chaonians were only included in the monarchic state of Epirus when King Pyrrhus came to power (297-272 BC) and the Epirote League became a powerful entity with stable royal control and great military potential (Cabanes 1976: 204). Some form of relations between Butrint and Molossia must have already existed, however, for the coast of Epirus was conquered by the Molossian kings, most notably by King Alketa (385-370 BC). In support of this notion, Dakaris highlights the fact that a group of Athenian soldiers crossed from Molossia to Corfu from the west coast of Epirus with Alketa's help after 373 BC (Dakaris 1964). This crossing is likely to have taken place from the bay of Butrint, the most suitable embarkation point because of both its natural features and the suburban city developed at that time. Moreover, based on an inscription of 370-368 BC found in Dodona, Dakaris argues that by this time the Molossians had invaded or brought under their influence most of Epirus, including Cassope, a

The 6th–2nd centuries BC: Archaic to Hellenistic structures 27

part or the whole of Thesprotia, Cestrina in the south of Chaonia, Trifilia and a part of western Macedonia (Dakaris 1964: 64).

The natural connection between Molossia and Butrint (Cestrina), the existence of appropriate ports in this area and its proximity to Corfu no doubt attracted the attention of King Alketa's successors, especially Alexander the Molossian and Pyrrhus, whose expansionist ambitions extended overseas. In his domestic policy Pyrrhus paid more attention than his predecessors to the development and fortification of existing towns as well as to the founding of new fortified towns, such as Antigoneia.

Pyrrhus must have also attended to the fortification of Butrint as an important coastal town. The cultural and socio-economic development that characterized the whole of Epirus from the end of the 4th century BC, and especially throughout the 3rd century BC, is reflected in the monuments and archaeological objects in Butrint. Two temples of this period have been preserved in Butrint: the temple of Asclepius; and the temple of Aphrodite, the latter being constructed at the end of the 3rd century BC and connected to the cult of Aphrodite that was brought by Pyrrhus to the towns of Epirus (cf. Plate 4).[2] Butrint is mentioned as one of the towns that embraced this cult. One of the temples is situated between the Theatre and the southern wall of the acropolis; here only the *cella* and the *pronaos* survive, while the front colonnade is missing. The other temple, reconstructed during the Roman period, had two columns in its façade and was supported by the western wall of the Theatre. In addition, a house, constructed with squared and polygonal blocks and dating from the 3rd century BC, survives near the Lake Gate (Plate 4). One of the most interesting and best-preserved monuments in Butrint is the Theatre (Plate 2), which was constructed in c. 230 BC on the southern slope of the acropolis. The *cavea* dates from this period. Thirteen rows of seats survive, constructed with blocks of skilfully carved stone that are separated into five sections by steps that served to admit spectators to the seating.

After Pyrrhus' death, and in particular after the death of his successor Alexander II in 240 BC, the move towards autonomy for Butrint and its suburbs must have gained momentum. The events of 230 BC (Phoenice's conquest by the Illyrians) did not affect Butrint. In fact, Butrint is not even mentioned in spite of its proximity and the presence of an Illyrian garrison camped on Corfu. Around this time a *koinon* was formed by the Prasaebians within the framework of the slave-owning republic of Epirus, the Epirote League (Cabanes 1976: 386). Material evidence for this lies in the construction of the Dema Wall, which was raised by the end of the

---

2 Editors note: the sanctuary and theatre area has recently been restudied and new dates and identifications have been attributed to certain monuments; see Gilkes 2003 and Hansen and Hodges 2007.

3rd century BC and divided Prasaebian territory from that of the Chaonians (Ceka 1976: 39) (Plate 3). To judge from previous events in the region around Butrint, the struggle for independence must have started even before the fall of the Epirote monarchy in 232 BC: with the rise of the Molossians from the end of the 5th century BC onwards Chaonia had become the principal region of Epirus. Phoenice, connected to the sea through the port of Onchesmos (modern Saranda), was the Epirote capital, and it is possible that Phoenice's promotion of Onchesmos spurred the Butrint area towards even greater independence.

Epigraphic studies by Faik Drini have determined that around the middle of the 2nd century BC the structure of Prasaebian organisation was transformed. The changes comprised a progression from the status of *koinon*, a component of a wider federal union (the Epirote League), to the status of an independent state. Butrint was the centre of the Prasaebian independent *koinon*. The extent of this *koinon*, while remaining part of the republic of Epirus, has been identified by Neritan Ceka in his study of Prasaebian fortifications (Ceka 1976). The territory included the land around Lake Butrint and was defined by both its natural borders and the fortifications that protected its entry points, such as the Dema Wall that formed its northern border (Ceka 1976). The formation of the Prasaebian *koinon* is suggested by Drini to have taken place no later than 172 BC; by 170 BC the Epirote League had been divided and ceased to exist. Butrint's political importance after 200 BC is suggested by the fact that significant individuals from Delphi travelled not only to Dodona and Cassope, but also to Phoenice and Butrint (Franke 1961: 111; cf. Daux 1949: 28). From 167 BC Epirus, Chaonia and a part of Thesprotia were clearly identified as Roman allies against Perseus of Macedonia, while ten years later a new distinction was made reflecting the Prasaebians' separation from Chaonia.

Unlike Molossia, Chaonia and a part of Thesprotia maintained a pro-Roman position based on their economic interests. The Prasaebians are likely to have adopted this pro-Roman position too, due to their seaward outlook, especially so after the Roman blockade of Corfu, the Ionian island to which the Prasaebians were traditionally linked by trade ties. However, in the later years of his reign Charops the Younger, once renowned as pro-Roman, fell out with Rome and as a result suffered a mysterious death in Brundisium in 157 BC. The reasons propounded by Polybius on this conflict are not convincing and other deeper reasons should be sought. Rome was not interested in bringing about the reunification of Epirus, a scheme at odds with her strategy of '*divide et impera*' (literally to 'divide and rule', but thereafter to unite culturally and politically under Roman authority). Rather, the Romans encouraged the Prasaebian struggle for autonomy until they afforded them the status of an independent *koinon* in *c.* 157

BC. Doubtless, the Romans must have been positively interested in strengthening the Prasaebian *koinon*, especially with regards to its defensive capability, in order to ensure a desirable equilibrium in the region.

The conference of formal independence was also granted to some Illyrian tribes who had assisted the Romans in their war against Macedonia. The Prasaebian independent *koinon*, with its centre in Butrint, was even more secure after 148 BC, when Epirus was included in the province of Macedonia. The Prasaebians, as shown by the inscriptions discovered in Butrint, preserved their particular administration until at least 100 BC. Almost the same thing happened to the *koinon* of the Epirotes, which appears to have been formed in 155 BC. This was not a unification of the whole of Epirus, as Cabanes supposes, but must have included the weakened Molossia and a part of Thesprotia. The title 'Epirote *koinon*', which evokes the former dominant rule of the Molossians, is indicative of Roman diplomacy in preserving some sort of regional power balance.

The issue of the founding of Butrint is an entirely separate subject. Principally because of its proximity to Corfu most scholars have considered it as a town founded by Greeks. This opinion has been disputed since the study of the inscriptions in the Theatre. Hasan Ceka was the first to demonstrate the difference between the Prasaebian institutions with their centre in Butrint and the institutions of the Greek colonies and towns even though the officials sometimes possessed Greek names (Ceka 1967: 244). Later, Pierre Cabanes, after studying the same inscriptions, noted that the population of Butrint and the area around it had entirely distinct customs from those of Greece proper (Cabanes 1976: 422). Forms of property ownership are one aspect that clearly distinguishes Epirus from central and southern Greece. The inscriptions that mention the freeing of slaves in Butrint show the continuity of the family in the ownership of property (Cabanes 1976: 339-444). Another feature is the special position of women, which differs from that in classical Greek cities in that they had full rights of ownership and could be the head of a family (Cabanes 1981: 62). A third characteristic is that society in Epirus was organized into various ethnic groupings, similar to neighbouring Illyrian communities, instead of being organized in *poleis*, which was a characteristic of central and southern Greece (Cabanes 1981: 63). The study of the ancient fortifications of this town, their new dating and the fact that none of the ancient historians talk of settlement by Greek colonists in Butrint draws us to the same conclusion as Cabanes.

The foundation of Butrint is mentioned in several ancient legends that attribute this event to Trojans in the aftermath of the destruction of Troy by the Greeks. In *The Aeneid* (3.193-505), Virgil recounts that the Trojan hero Aeneas, before journeying to Italy to raise the walls of a new Troy, stopped in Butrint where he met Helenus, the son of Priam, king of Troy, who had been brought to Butrint as a slave. According to Virgil, he had constructed a fortress at Butrint that resembled his home city. Another version of the legend is told by Teucros of Cyzicus (1st century BC) (quoted by Stephanus Byzantinus *Ethnica* s.v. "Buthrotos"). In this account, upon reaching the coast of Epirus Helenus decided to make a customary sacrifice to the gods. Having received an initial wound, the bull selected for the offering leapt into the water and, after swimming for some time across the bay, reached the opposite shore where it died from its injuries. This incident was interpreted by Helenus as an instruction from the gods to found a city on that spot and name it Buthrotum in respect of the event.

There is no archaeological evidence whatsoever to support a Trojan foundation of the city of Butrint even though the idea that Trojans colonised Epirus after the destruction of Troy was widely accepted in antiquity and is referred to by several ancient authors, including Dionysius of Halicarnassus (2.51.2). He reports the presence of Trojans in Thessaly, Epirus and in the vicinity of Butrint. However, despite frequent references to the settlement of Trojans in or near Butrint, nothing is said about the foundation of the city by Greek colonists, unlike other towns on the Albanian coastline such as the small town of Oricum. Butrint's inclusion amongst the cities that considered themselves to have been founded by the heroes of Greek mythology does not distinguish it from the rest of Epirus; in fact, ethnically, it links it even more closely to Epirus. Furthermore, the legend of Butrint's founding is directly linked to that of the descent of the Molossian royal dynasty from Neoptolemus, the son of Achilles and Andromache, the widow of the Trojan hero Hector; this legend was widely known in Epirus by the 5th century BC (Dakaris 1964). The myth of the founding of Butrint was developed relatively late in comparison to the legends of the mythological descent of the Molossian royal family and must belong to the time that the southern part of Chaonia and Cestrina fell under Molossian control, which probably took place in the first quarter of the 5th century BC (Dakaris 1964: 64). Later, Pyrrhus used his own ancestral myth and cult to the service of his expansionist policies (Dakaris 1964: 166).

The acceptance of this myth on the part of the Buthrotians shows their non-Greek character, though this view differs from that of Dakaris regarding the Greek origins of the Epirote tribes (Dakaris 1964: 267). This issue has been well explained by Nilsson who writes that: 'This attribution of mythical names is in contradiction to the principles of the onomatology of the Classical period, during which the living were never named after famous heroes. This affair shows the endeavours of a barbarian family to represent itself as Greek heroes' and that '...the Epirotes were trying to show through this exaltation that they were administering a foreign property that they didn't know how to use' (Nilsson 1909; 1951: 108).

Another example from the Illyrian lands that border northern Chaonia supports this conclusion. With the extension of Pyrrhus' rule as far as Apollonia, the inhabitants of the Illyrian town of Byllis, not far from Apollonia, embraced the genealogical legend of the Molossians, attributing the founding of the town to Neoptolemus and even using this heroic figure on coins minted there around 260 BC (Stephanus Byzantinus *Ethnica* s.v. "Buthrotos"; Ceka 1965: 81). Such a phenomenon did not occur in neighbouring Apollonia or in the small town of Oricum. These communities attributed the founding of their towns to colonists from Euboea (according to Pseudo-Scymnus 441-443) and Chalcis (according to Pliny *Natural History* 3.23). This proves that local people still remembered the origins of the foundation of these towns, and did not link it to the names of mythological heroes in a manner that at that time would have constituted a break with Greek custom. If we were to suppose that Butrint was founded by Greek colonists from, say Corfu or Corinth, it would be difficult to rationalise their settlement being so close to the large fortified prehistoric centres of Kalivo, Vagalat, and Karalibej (cf. Plate 3). It seems though that Butrint was also assisted in becoming a city by its natural and economic situations. Although at first it may have been merely a trading centre connecting its hinterland to Corfu, Butrint appears to have formed an economic structure that distinguished it from the settlements around it.

From this survey of the few and fragmentary historical sources, it seems that Butrint grew to be the centre for an entire region. At the end of the 6th century BC, it was the only city mentioned in this area. At the same time, or a little later, it emerged as an independent city linked to the *peiraia* of Corfu. Then, by the final 30 years of the 3rd century BC it developed as an economic, political, and administrative centre for the Prasaebian tribe, first within the framework of the Epirote League and later as an independent entity. In this later period Butrint and the area around it experienced the same troubles and insecurities as the rest of Epirus, conditioned by the interests of the great powers of the time, such as the Illyrian, Macedonian and Roman states. Furthermore, Butrint, from what can be understood from its defensive structures, also had to confront the ambitions of its nearest neighbours both before, and especially after, 157 BC. This complex situation is reflected to a certain degree in the town's fortifications, in the diverse stages of construction, in the destruction and reconstruction of the walls, as well as in the extension or reduction of the town's fortified area according to the requirements of the time.

THE DEFENSIVE WALLS

One of the main challenges concerning the fortifications of Butrint is to determine their development through time. The absence of surviving structures in many parts of the defensive circuit has resulted in conflicting interpretations being proposed by different researchers, as discussed in the preceding chapter on the previous studies on Butrint. For the arrangement of the fortification walls during the pre-Roman period, the different interpretations may be summarised as follows.

Ugolini proposes three chronologically distinct circuit walls in Butrint. The earliest circuit was on the upper platform of the acropolis hill; the second (polygonal) circuit was half way up the hill; and the third was at the foot of the hill. Other researchers from the Italian mission naturally concur with this opinion. Hammond accepts only one defensive circuit in Butrint, the lower one, and considers the other walls to have been retaining or terracing walls, a view Neritan Ceka disagrees with. Instead Ceka sides with Ugolini in believing that the upper platform of the hill was indeed surrounded by a wall. Regarding the proposed second-phase wall, Ceka agrees with Ugolini in seeing it is a defensive structure, but disagrees with him on the form of its plan. Ceka does not accept the wall above the Theatre as a separate circuit and links it to the lower circuit on the east side of the Tower Gate (Plate 5). Of the three, Ceka's argument seems to be the most persuasive, but with a few amendments: the wall that connects the Lake Gate to the acropolis, which Ceka placed in 'Butrint IV' (seeing it as belonging to the same period as the Tower Gate and the second phase of the Lion Gate), in fact belongs to a much later period as we shall discuss later. The same thing may be said for the section marked K-L on Ceka's plan.

Therefore, for the prehistoric and the earliest ancient periods, we can only suppose that there was a circuit on the upper platform of the acropolis hill with a second, later one that passed along its foot on the north and east sides and half way down the hill on the south side. Ultimately, we have an extension to the fortification on the south side in the flatter area at the base of the hill. If we examine it in plan, the new south wall is set 40 m distant from the earlier one, and runs for a length of 260 m. The upper fortification, on the acropolis, covered 0.4 ha, while the lower one enclosed 4 ha, with the surrounding walls 870 m in length. In place of towers, shallow rectangular, wide-fronted bastions were employed, which are distinct from towers in that they are internally filled and are of the same height as the adjoining walls. The same role was played by the zigzag turns that the wall line followed. In general, the walls have a width of 2.60–3.80 m and were constructed with carefully worked massive stones displayed on the outer faces, while the inner parts of the walls were filled with rubble. The walls have different styles and techniques of construction, which in many cases belie their origins in different periods of time.

STYLES AND TECHNIQUES OF CONSTRUCTION

In defining the styles and chronology of walls in Butrint we should bear in mind their essential differences within given time periods, and we must also be aware of disparate elements when a wall contains constituents from several different periods.

The earliest traces of the walls of Butrint are to be seen on the acropolis. Around the midpoint of the southern acropolis wall, two lengths of wall constructed with un-worked stones and without mortar can be seen; the blocks are relatively large and have voids between them (Plates 6-7). The eastern of these two sections belongs to an almost right-angled turn in the circuit wall, while the other section to the west comes immediately after a turn in the medieval wall which itself seems to follow the line of the ancient walls. Ugolini identified only one of these sections and named it a 'pelasgic' wall. The technique used in these walls may be defined as belonging to the 'broken stones, set without mortar' type. To the west of these sections another 4 m long stretch of wall is preserved; the external faces of the blocks have been left un-worked as they came from the quarry, but their sides have been scored to achieve a better join between blocks (Plate 8). The stones vary in length from 0.50-1.20 m and are typically 0.40-0.70 m high. Ugolini considered this wall to belong to the 'primitive polygonal' type. Further east there is a section of wall in the polygonal style (Plate 9); the blocks are substantial and up to 2.40 m long x 1 m high. The stones have been worked with a hammer to create flat faces and the joins, too, have received careful attention. In all the walls described above only their outer face can be seen, while in the interior of the acropolis the ground surface is higher and walls of the Roman and medieval periods are supported on these sections making it impossible to assess the earliest constructions in more detail. In conclusion, we can say that on the acropolis there are two main periods of construction which, according to their style and technique, can be further assigned to one of three phases: construction with 'broken stones'; mortar-free construction; and polygonal construction. The earliest period is represented by two phases of construction, the second of which is distinguished by a better jointing of the blocks and is similar to the construction technique of the walls on Kalivo.

The second circuit at Butrint, made from large blocks of ashlar masonry, represents the main building phase of defensive structures at Butrint in the pre-Roman period. The north wall of the acropolis does not preserve any prehistoric or antique traces, although it is possible that its stones were reworked and reused in the new circuit. This circuit starts with the section above the Theatre that is constructed in the polygonal style (Plate 10). In contrast to the polygonal section on the southern wall of the acropolis, the blocks here are smaller and more compact and in placing the stones emphasis is given to stylistic effect over stability. It is clear that the mason mastered the technique of building dry walls so thoroughly that he was able to play with it to create the required effects. This style can be seen in almost identical form in Lissus and Çuka e Ajtoit and temporally coincides with the extension of the defensive structures at these centres and the increasing economic prosperity of the area at that time. Scranton has pointed out a distinctive feature within the polygonal style, that of the alignment of blocks that are almost rectangular (Scranton 1941: 52) (cf. Plate 13). He calls this style 'aligned polygonal', which, in contrast to the authentic polygonal style, is a product of the Hellenistic period. The same term was used by Ceka to describe the polygonal walls at Butrint and Lissus (Ceka 1976: 27-33). Clear examples of this kind of wall are few, however, while in most cases it is confused with the genuine polygonal, even where block alignment does not assume all the features of the Hellenistic period polygonal. Thus, it would be fairer to use the term 'late polygonal' or 'Hellenistic polygonal' for a construction technique in which a tendency for stylistic effects can be seen. Nevertheless, it is often difficult, and sometimes impossible, to see the difference between the early and late polygonal. This is partly because the varying skills of masons and the financial means available in different centres perpetuated a widespread tendency to replicate older styles. For reasons already outlined, it is difficult to date a wall simply on the basis of its polygonal style, except in very specific and typical cases. This is one of the main reasons why some scholars have entirely repudiated the stylistic classification of Scranton and thus overlooked some of its more enduring aspects (Beschi 1968).

Accordingly, in the section above the Theatre we encounter a 'late polygonal' style wall that was built contemporaneously with the main city walls constructed in the style represented at the Lake Gate. The inability to define an accurate chronology of this style brought Ugolini to the mistaken conclusion that these were the ruins of a distinct circuit in Butrint halfway up the hill (Ugolini 1942: 26). Meanwhile Hammond's notion that these sections were terracing walls was based on the absence of an internal face (Hammond 1967: 100-1). A part of this wall was destroyed when the Theatre was constructed in order to extend the *cavea*, so it can no longer be traced without interruption. The circuit wall from this period is best preserved on the north side where it reaches a height of 5 m and a width of 3.80 m. At certain points stones were placed with their longest axis vertical. To the north and east two main construction styles are evident. The first style is best characterized by the Lake Gate where the stones in the façade are trapezoidal and roughly dressed by hammer; the adjoining faces of the blocks have multiple indentations. The second style is chiefly represented by the Lion Gate where regular rectangular blocks are laid in parallel courses and indentations are less frequent. The outer surfaces of the stones protrude and have been roughly hammered. The height of the courses is not uniform and, even though this phenomenon does not follow any certain rule, one cannot fail to notice the influence of the rectangular pseudo-isodomic style. In the walls near (cf. Plate 13) and in the Lake Gate (despite these being generally similar to those of the Tower Gate) stones are not set vertically to tie courses together, and it is possible that this type was only used for the relatively thinner walls of the towers. In the north fortification wall there is a small polygonal section that is connected with a section of the trapezoidal type that Ugolini labels 'pseudo-polygonal'. Hammond terms it 'real polygonal' and considers it to be a repair of an early wall of the Lake Gate type. Both agree that this small polygonal section is not of the same period as the walls nearby.

Having established that the wall above the Theatre belongs to the 'late polygonal' style on the basis of a number of stylistic criteria, this small trapezoidal section further strengthens our conviction that in Butrint, as at Lissus, there is a simultaneous combination of polygonal and trapezoidal styles. A contemporaneous mixture of styles can also be found in the lower city wall west of the Theatre where the polygonal combines naturally with the quadrangular style (Plate 11). Further west the wall is only quadrangular whilst other separate sections of polygonal also exist (Plate 12).

Ugolini records that the walls of the Lake Gate type have 'as many as six or seven corners', while Hammond claims they belong to 'a variant of the quadrangular type' (Ugolini 1942: 44; Hammond 1967) (Plate 14). In a previous study these walls were defined as belonging to the 'aligned trapezoidal' style, but later Ceka calls them 'trapezoidal with a broken alignment' (Ceka 1976: 31). Staying with the term 'aligned trapezoidal' we notice not only that it is contemporary with 'late polygonal', but also that the two often intermesh in the same wall thereby forming a kind of mixed style. The most typical examples of this can be found at Lissus and Çuka e Ajtoit (Prendi and Zheku 1972). The style with rectangular blocks in parallel courses may be defined as 'rectangular with pseudo-isodomic tendencies' and may be contemporary with, or later than, the 'aligned trapezoidal'. Hence it may be contemporary in the Lake Gate but of a later period in the Tower Gate; further, it is possible that this style may have continued in use over a relatively long period. Ultimately, in order to solve this problem once and for all, investigations need to be conducted in a number of places.

Diverse construction styles and techniques may also be noted in the wall that runs southwest from the Tower Gate. This wall undoubtedly belongs to the last period of the ancient defensive network. It was constructed at a time when there was a need to include a number of public and religious buildings to the south of the hillside within the circuit, particularly the temple and the Theatre, as the construction of the latter had affected the existing defensive wall. Various construction techniques can be seen in the wall in the area of the Theatre, but in general it was constructed with large rectangular or trapezoidal blocks in isodomic rows, with a width of 2.45 m and a height of almost 0.50 m. The west part of this wall was constructed with vertical stones every 3 m that project on the inside to form pilasters (0.86 x 0.82 m). By and large, the wall was constructed with re-used blocks. This can also be determined from the variety of work on the outer faces of the stones in a single section of wall. Its construction corresponds chronologically with the reconstruction of the wall to the east of the Tower Gate, where the re-used blocks of the second period are of the same dimension and form as those in the wall at the west end of the lower circuit.

THE GATES

The gates in the city wall are of particular interest because of their structural design as well as the degree of their preservation. There were six entrances into the ancient town of which only two survive in very good condition: the Lake Gate on the northeast side, and the Lion Gate further to the west on the north side (Plate 4).

The Lake Gate

This monumental gate is situated on the northeast side of the lower circuit wall leaving only a narrow (8.50 m wide) apron of land between the gate and the lake. It has a concealed entrance and a covered passageway partly within the width of the wall. The southeast side of the gate is protected by a 2 m long offset of the encircling wall (Plates 14-16). The gate is 4 m high and 1.50 m wide. The surviving height on the inside of the fortification is 2.10 m. The passage walls are not parallel and at the inner end of the passage there is a U-shaped indent in the southeast wall that is not matched in the wall opposite (Fig. 1). The covered part of the gateway is 5.25 m long and is roofed with a monolithic stone ceiling that is supported on each side by stone consoles with curved undersides (Plate 15). To provide greater stability, the ceiling is partly carried by the side walls of the passageway, thus distributing the weight of the wall above the passageway more evenly.

The 6th–2nd centuries BC: Archaic to Hellenistic structures

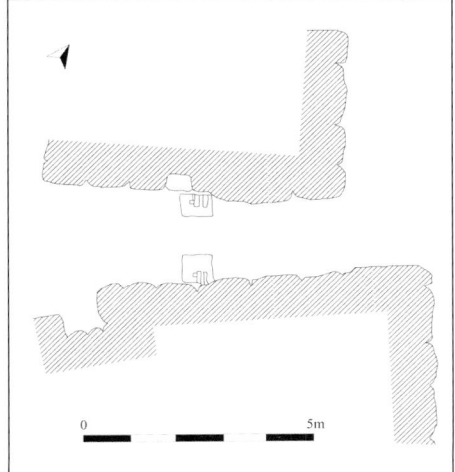

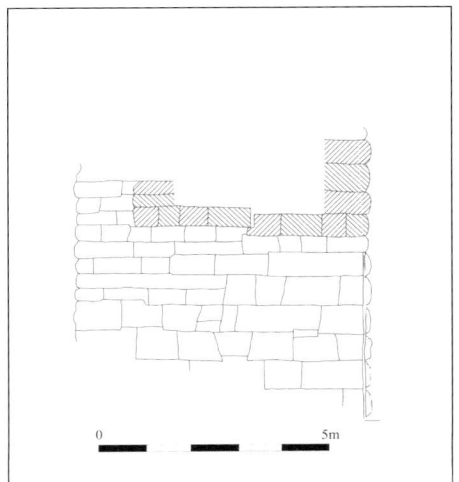

Fig. 1 The Lake Gate, plan of internal steps and gate fitting

Fig. 2 The Lake Gate interior, southeast-facing elevation

The passage floor ascends as it enters the city, paralleled by a change in ceiling height corresponding to a step in the floor. The entranceway is thus divided into two parts, the section nearest the exterior deliberately set 0.18 m lower than the inner section to emphasize the effect of reduced height and space towards the interior. On the upper side of the step opposed stone blocks on either side of the passage bear cuts to receive the gateway door posts. In this way, if the doors were forced, the occupants would be striking from an advantageous height. The narrow passage would limit the number of potential attackers entering from outside, while the open area to the rear of the passage would allow a great number of defenders.

In contrast to the Lion Gate, described below, the door of the Lake Gate was not positioned in its façade, but set halfway into the passageway. Here, as well as the indented threshold stones, grooves that admitted a doorframe are visible in both side walls. In respect of the in-passage position of the door and the offset exterior wall, the Lake Gate is very similar to the gates at Lissus. However, at Lissus the inner passageway was not roofed. The covered passage of the Lake Gate would lend some cover to would-be assaults on the doors. This issue was negated, however, because the proximity of the lake in front of gate would have made the use of a battering ram or other machinery difficult. Moreover, the 2 m offset of the southeast exterior wall served to control the approach to the gate whilst also concealing it from the most likely direction of attack.

The façade of the gate is constructed with large trapezoidal stone blocks, roughly worked with a hammer; rabbeting has been used to fit the blocks together. The dimensions of the blocks vary from 0.90-1.20 m long x 0.65-0.70 m high. In the upper part of the entrance smaller blocks only 0.50 m high were included. In the inner half of the passageway the construction style changes: the stones are universally smaller and rectangular, and rabbeting is more rarely employed (Fig. 2). This change of style was cited by Ugolini as evidence for a southwards extension to the passage in a later phase, perhaps a century after its original construction (Ugolini 1942: 57). Ugolini based his argument on the following observations:

1. Stone blocks in the upper courses of the passageway walls are smaller than in the lower courses and less frequently rabbeted.
2. The corner stones at the angle of the entrance are deeply cut, whereas those at the internal corners are not.
3. The corbel blocks in the upper level (to the south) of the ceiling are less strong than those in the lower level and the curvature of the former is more flat.

The Italian's interpretation was rejected by Hammond, though, who claimed that all elements of the gate were conceived as a single construction (Hammond 1967: 102-3). Hammond explains the difference in the dimensions of the blocks by the need for greater strength in the walls in the part of the passageway nearest the entrance, the point where battering rams would most likely be applied. According to Hammond, rabbeting is also a feature that adds to the strength of a wall, while the cutting of the corner stones, quite usual in fortifications in Epirus, is almost always found only on the outer faces of an entrance. We might add that this feature could also be explained as being part of the construction style of a wall that is later than most scholars have thought, as will be discussed in detail below.

The Lion Gate
The Lion Gate is formed at a break and shift in the line of the city wall, creating a partial overlap of the two wall lines and producing a passageway between them (Fig. 3). As in the Lake Gate, the passage is roofed and is 3.40 m high x 2.15 m wide at the exterior, and 2.90 m wide at the interior. The current entrance is 1.19 m wide x 1.50 m high – the result of a later phase of construction in which the entrance was made narrower by the positioning of a monolithic block on the south side with smaller but still substantial blocks stacked on the north. A second monolithic block was used as an architrave on which a depiction of a lion devouring a bull's head, inspired by a scene from Archaic Greek art, was carved in

The 6th–2nd centuries BC: Archaic to Hellenistic structures

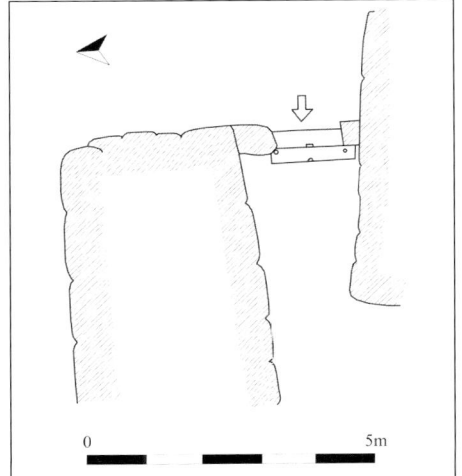

Fig. 3 The Lion Gate

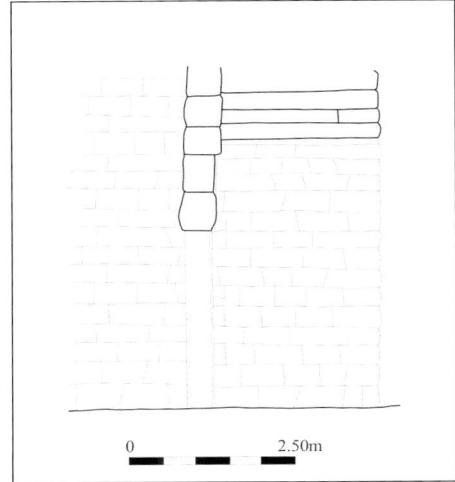

Fig. 4 The Lion Gate interior, north-facing elevation

shallow relief (Plate 17). Above the architrave is another row of blocks that in-fill the remainder of the original entrance (Fig. 4). Based on technical observations, Ugolini concluded that the restriction of the entrance is a later addition. He notes that the monolith on the south side of the gate is completely detached from the wall, while the stones on the north are very large, reused and do not match those on the north side of the passageway to the rear. It is clear that the architrave with the figure of the lion is a later addition because the south wall of the entrance has been reduced by a few centimetres to accommodate it (Ugolini 1942: 63).

The ceiling over the passage was constructed in the same way as that of the Lake Gate, with profiled consoles protruding from the side walls by 0.30 m, supporting stones that are also partly carried by the flanking walls. Thus, even if the consoles were to break at some point, the ceiling would not collapse. The consoles, unlike those in the Lake Gate, are roughly profiled with diagonal-cut edges. Above the ceiling there is a row of profiled stones (Fig. 5) at both ends on which a second ceiling was supported. Ugolini was able to identify this detail through a break in the lower ceiling. Thus, a

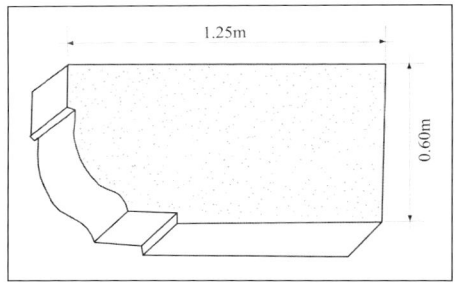

Fig. 5 The Lion Gate, detail of roof console

double ceiling, with a void between, was created (Fig. 6). This manner of construction relieved the great weight of the wall directly above the entrance from the consoles, throwing it on to the upper ceiling and the side walls of the passageway instead.

During restoration works carried out on the Lion Gate in 1962, it was recorded that the space between the two rows of the architrave was trapezoidal in shape, with the longest side at the bottom, thus part of the wall's weight would be borne by the side walls of the gate (Zheku 1971: 81). Hammond (1967: 104-5) suggests another motive for these technical features:

> The object of introducing a double ceiling, which must be original in the building of the gateway, is presumably to conceal the upper ceiling, which is in fact structural; the reason for so concealing it springs from the need to deceive an attacking force. For if one had to assault such a gateway with a battering ram one would aim first at the (apparently) weakest point of the structure, namely the monolithic architrave resting on its slim corbels. From the outside of the wall one would, however, be seeing the false architrave, that is, the first monolith forming the lower ceiling, and the smashing of that architrave would not result in collapsing the main wall above, which is supported by the upper concealed ceiling.

Further, Hammond believed that the second phase of the gate, the narrowed entrance, was built as a response to the deception of the double ceiling having been exposed and broken by an assault. The new façade was consequently designed to once more conceal the gap between the two ceilings with a new false architrave, that with the lion relief. Reducing the entrance of the Lion Gate in ancient times did not present problems, because neither this gate nor the Lake Gate were ever used for the movement of wheeled vehicles, but only for pedestrians and cavalry because of the terrain and the inclusion of steps or stairs (Plate 18). Nonetheless, both Ugolini and Zheku date the reconstruction of the gate to late antiquity. However, considering the use of mortar, it seems more likely that the reconstruction took place in the 1st century AD during the reign of the Emperor Augustus.

If one disregards its architectural details and layout, the Lion Gate would appear to be one of the earliest types of ancient entrances. However, it is plain from its passageway – which is both broader and shorter – that it belongs to a later phase than the Lake Gate. Unlike the Lake Gate, the door of the Lion Gate was situated at the front of the passage, rather than in the middle. The evidence for this lies in a pair of opposed grooves on the side walls of the entrance that served to fix the gate frame. This frontal positioning of the door makes good sense considering the very different aspect that this gate presents in comparison to the Lake Gate.

Moreover, the Lion Gate was constructed in a different style to the Lake Gate. The blocks of stone are smaller, 0.30-0.50 m high x 0.60-0.70 m long, and are placed in parallel courses with no rabbeting. The north wall of the passageway is preserved to a height of 11 courses to the rear of

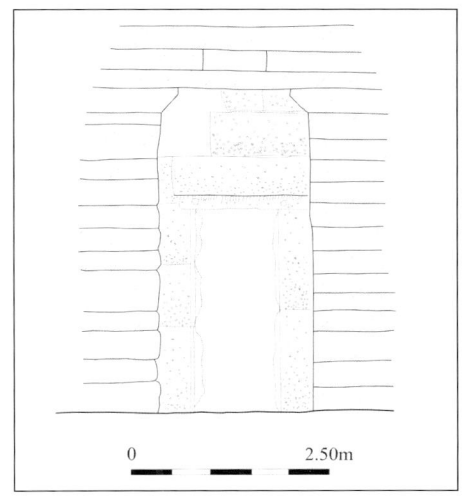

Fig. 6 The Lion Gate, west-facing (interior) elevation

the gateway, of which the five lowest courses are made up of smaller blocks than those above. The faces of the stones have been worked with a hammer. The same style is witnessed on the south side of the passageway, especially in the section of wall to the east of the gate that is the continuation of the south passageway wall, except that here the rows of stone are isodomic (Plate 19). The style used on the inner face of the north wall of the passage (Plate 20) is the same as that of the U-shaped tower that protects the entrance on the southeast side of the town (the Tower Gate). The difference in the style of construction from the remainder of the gate poses the question as to whether the Lion Gate itself is of the same period as the Lake Gate. All previous academics have expressed this doubt but have given different answers to the question: Ugolini was content in defining this as a later period of construction; Hammond was more hesitant; while Ceka was of the opinion that only the wall on the south side of the entrance was reconstructed.

Ceka's interpretation can be disputed on a number of counts. Firstly, the collapse of the south wall would destroy the entire gate except for the consoles on the north side, but these, as seen today, are no different from those on the south side. Secondly, the wall would not collapse completely down to ground level. Thirdly, the style of construction is the same not only for the two walls of the passageway, but also for a large part of the wall outside the entrance. If a later style were present here then we would see an entirely new gate along with a part of the city wall beside it. To counter this argument, the outer face of the wall on the north side of the passageway would need to be studied although, unfortunately, this has collapsed and has been filled with mortared stones at a much later period. To assess the lower part of this wall would require extensive excavation. Nevertheless, it is probable that the gate was indeed remodelled at a much later date when the circuit walls were comprehensively rebuilt (Plate 21).

The North Gate

The North Gate is situated on the northwest extent of the wall circuit between the Lion Gate and the West Gate. It was excavated by Ugolini and is less well preserved than the other gates. It has a passageway 5.50 m long x 2.40 m wide formed by a shift in the line of the circuit walls in the same manner as the Lion Gate. The stone blocks forming the gate are 0.85-1.30 m long x 0.35-0.55 m high. This was one of the largest gates, sufficiently wide to admit wheeled vehicles. The scale of the North Gate is evident not only from the width of the entrance passage, but also from a console found here which is larger than the those in either the Lake Gate or the Lion Gate (Ugolini 1942: 65). The console measures 1.25 x 0.60 m and has been carefully profiled on the inside, in contrast to the consoles of the other gates. This quality does not imply that the console belongs to a different period from those of the Lake Gate, but simply that the size and importance of the North Gate entrance necessitated larger components to bear the additional weight they had to support.

The West Gate

The West Gate (Plate 22) is similar in design to the Lake Gate. As in the latter, the wall line is offset to the northwest, projecting 2.15 m from the front of the entrance. This afforded the occupants better control over the approach to the gate. The lower courses of blocks on the northwest side of the gate are very similar to those of the Lake Gate, while the upper element of the wall is comprised of narrow blocks, *c.* 0.35 m high, in neat courses with no rabbeting to join them together. The southeast side of the West Gate has been reconstructed with blocks in isodomic courses, but the finishing of their outer faces varies considerably and it is therefore evident that they have been reused from other structures.

The Asclepieion Gate

The Asclepieion Gate is situated near the Theatre, towards the west end of the southern, lower encircling walls. Originally, the gate was designed as a simple entrance. At a later point an inner courtyard was added to it, of which only a part, including the remains of a covered entrance with a semicircular arch, survives (Plate 23). There is no surviving evidence to suggest how the original entrance was roofed, but it is quite possible that the entrance had a semicircular arch that would be perfectly in keeping with a wall with pilasters as seen to the north of the entrance. The lower encircling wall contains numerous pilasters and is constructed in a variety of styles (Plates 24-28).

The Tower Gate

A second entrance, the Tower Gate (Plate 29), is situated at the opposite end of the south fortification wall to the Asclepieion Gate. So-named by Pirro Marconi, who first excavated here, it is the only entrance in Butrint protected by two towers. Of the two towers, that on the northeast side is U-shaped whilst the other is square. The towers are separated by a passageway 2.85 m wide (Fig. 7). The former tower projects further from the circuit wall with an overall length of 15.55 m and width of 8.23 m, while the latter tower has maximum dimensions of 3.95 x 3.95 m.

The passageway between the two towers is 7 m long. At the front of the passage there was a moveable gate (portcullis) and the grooves in which this was carried are still visible on both sides of the passage. The portcullis was set just inside (0.70 m) the entranceway. A second gate was set further towards the rear of the passageway. Its position is betrayed by a 0.20 x 0.20 m hole to receive a door bolt. Each tower is pierced by an arrow slit facing into the passage between the two gates. The towers' other slits all face outwards.

The U-shaped tower is divided by a wall into two smaller spaces that communicate via a centrally placed door. In the middle of each space there is a

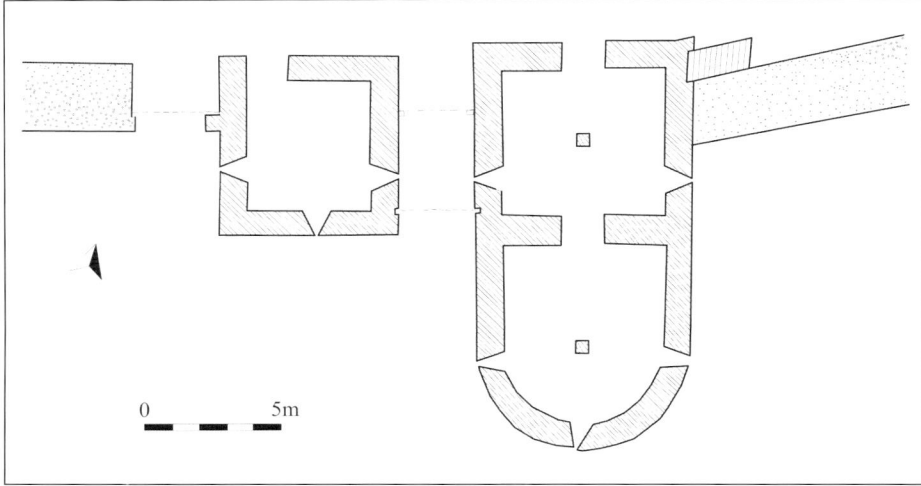

Fig. 7 The Tower Gate

Fig. 8 The Tower Gate, reconstruction drawing (Instituti i Arkeologjisë)

stone column that supported the floor beams of an upper storey (Plates 30-31). The walls of both towers are 1 m wide, that is, the thickness of two blocks. At certain points individual blocks extend across the whole width of the wall to provide greater strength to the structure. The U-shaped tower walls were constructed with rectangular blocks in courses of unequal height, displaying a tendency towards the pseudo-isodomic style. The outer faces of the stones have been roughly worked with a hammer and rabbeting is used only rarely. The U-shaped tower walls are similar to the north side of the Lion Gate passage. The blocks in the external wall face of the square tower are taller, which compounds its less secure form against attack.

Following the excavation of this entrance by Marconi and its graphic reconstruction, the Tower Gate was studied by Frederick Winter (Winter 1971: 264). He described it as a gate that employs a portcullis as an integral element of the outer line of defences, whilst the second gate served to control access to the passageway. Beside their tactical use to attract and then help eliminate small groups of attackers, portcullises worked to protect an ordinary gate behind. Winter adhered to the 3rd century BC dating of the Tower Gate put forward by Marconi, but he could only find two examples of a portcullis from the Hellenistic period. One of these is the Tower Gate itself, while all other available examples and literary evidence date from the Roman period (Winter 1971: 264). Nevertheless, because of 'the practical character of the Hellenistic military architecture' and 'the technical insight of the Hellenic engineers', Winter concluded that the use of movable gates in this period must have been far more widespread (Winter 1971: 264).

Guri Pani (1976) provides a full description of the Tower Gate in an article in *Monumentet*, drawing attention to the location of the portcullis and adding a row of windows on the upper storey to Marconi's reconstruction (Fig. 8). During his survey he also discovered a second entrance, adjacent to the square tower on its west side. The main gates, as well as the tower door, were covered by a wooden screen. Pani dates the Tower Gate to the beginning of the 3rd century BC, later than the walls of Lake Gate type, simply because of the fact that the gate is not tied in to the wall to the northeast (Pani 1976).

Assuming that the elongated U-shaped tower was built to control the secondary entrance as well as the passageway entrance, Ceka considers the two to be contemporary and integral elements in the design of the gateway. On the other hand, Ceka does not exclude the possibility that the U-shaped form was designed to distribute the weight of the tower's defensive architecture (Ceka 1976: 32, note 20). However, this would not actually have been an issue, as the towers were not covered by arches but only by a wooden roof: arches would not have been appropriate for such thin tower walls. The excavation of the wall to the southwest of the Tower Gate was carried out by Kosta Lako (Lako 1981: 29). Based on the data retrieved from this excavation, a later date was ascribed to the southwest wall than to the Tower Gate itself. Similar to the arrangement at the Lion Gate, a stone pilaster on the west face of the square tower acts as a doorframe for the entrance but is not integral to the tower wall, whereas in the wall to the southwest the door frame is integral to the wall.

The Tower Gate, together with the wall to its southwest, is dated by Ceka to Butrint IV, around the end of the 3rd century BC, as a construction brought about by the events of 230 BC when the Illyrian state captured Phoenice and stationed a military garrison on Corfu (Ceka 1976: 39). The wall immediately northeast of the Tower Gate (Plate 32) is dated earlier by Ceka to Butrint III.

THE DEMA WALL

The Dema Wall should be seen as an intrinsic part of the fortified system of Butrint and its distinctive character is of great interest. This wall traversed the Ksamil peninsula at its narrowest point and controlled the route along the coastline to Butrint (Plate 3). The wall begins at the shore of Lake Butrint, ascends up the hillside to the west and thereafter descends to the Ionian Sea (Plate 36). It measures between 9.20-9.60 m wide and comprises two parallel 2.80 m wide walls surrounding a 5 m thick core. Every 3-4 m the parallel walls were connected by lateral blocks. In order to provide sufficient space for steps to the upper levels, in some parts the wall was reduced to a width of around 7 m. The wall is made from large rectangular ashlars with flat faces. Each course is generally 0.80 m high, but in some cases the ashlars are up to 2.50 m long x 1.50 m high.

This fortification was not merely a wall closing off the Ksamil peninsula, but it also served as a defensive structure in its own right; in other words, it was effectively a castle. The wide upper walkway provided enough room for troops as well as for heavy catapults. The upper wall was surrounded by a parapet with firing loops, enabling it to be defended from the rear, too. The construction method, utilising two close parallel walls of large ashlars tied together by linking lateral blocks and with a stone-filled core, made the Dema Wall strong enough to withstand attack from heavy projectiles. At each end, next to the sea and the lake, the final blocks were worked into the hillside to prevent them from sliding down the slope and the ends of the wall were closed with facing stones with the same purpose.

DATING THE WALLS

As the historical sources are of little help and secure archaeological data are few, we must try to date the different phases of the walls by their architectural style and construction technique. The south walls of the acropolis, built from quarry stones without any bonding material, do not offer any technical data for precision dating. The only elements that might offer an absolute date are the zigzag line of the wall and the rudimentary way of working the stones to permit their connection.

Angles created by zigzag lines could also serve as towers, and this is a feature employed in late prehistoric fortifications. In Greece this system was first used during the 8th and 7th centuries BC, but was only widely used during the 5th century BC (Scranton 1941: 149-58). In Butrint there are archaeological remains from the 8th and 7th centuries BC. The zigzag line encountered in the prehistoric fortification of the acropolis is dated by archaeological evidence to the 7th century BC. This notwithstanding, the rudimentary way of working the stones to level the courses is not common in all prehistoric fortifications, but only in examples that have a later date confirmed by other structural features. Based on the dates of occupation on the acropolis and the technical features of the walls we would probably date these defensive structures to the 7th-6th centuries BC, and consider them to have been built in two separate phases.

Ceka dates the defensive system at Butrint to before the 4th century BC based on its resemblance to the polygonal wall at Amantia, which is considered to date from this period, in spite of the fact that it is acknowledged as one of the most difficult examples to date (Ceka 1976: 29). Flattened facing, which is rarely used in the polygonal style either in Albania or in Greece, is applied to wall sections at both sites. However, differences between them are obvious. In the polygonal wall at Butrint the stones are kept in place by their own weight and have uneven surfaces, while their linking courses are not particularly tidy. In Amantia, on the other hand, aesthetic effects are in evidence with carefully worked stone surfaces and the linking courses forming a complicated pattern that would not have been easy to construct and which, judging by the cross-cut stones, was very labour intensive. The configuration and shapes of the stone blocks was influenced by the Lesbian style. Amantia's polygonal wall has all the characteristics of the polygonal wall type distinctive of western Greece, and so it should be dated, according to Scranton's classification, to around the middle of the 5th century BC (Scranton 1941: 45-58). However, the same aesthetic effect was also maintained during the Hellenistic period. This seems to make it difficult to date not only a specific 'old fashioned' style, but also any other styles. Another common feature, other than the imitation of earlier styles, was the co-existence of different styles within a single architectural feature. The wall in question at Amantia is assigned to the later period of the polygonal style or to the Hellenistic period from the fact that the polygonal ashlars gradually became quadrangular with flat faces. In such cases, the latest style could be used to date the wall if it offered sufficient characteristic information; otherwise the mixed style could be used. In addition, in the polygonal style at Amantia the stones have oblique-cut edges, which is a characteristic of the Hellenistic period. It is no coincidence that in the dating of the polygonal walls at Acarnania and Aetolia, most of which are categorised in the mixed construction style, there has been a long debate as to whether they should be dated to the 5th or 3rd century BC. The quadrangular style with flat faces, widely used in Amantia, follows the quadrangular style with quarried or hammered stones in the chronology of Illyrian walls, so this wall cannot be earlier than the 3rd century BC.

Considering the fact that the polygonal style is widely used over a long period of time and that Scranton's classification of this style is ineffective, it would be difficult to date the polygonal wall on the Butrint acropolis by stylistic criteria. Instead, we should place it in time between the acropolis walls with rough quarried stones and the Lake Gate, thus giving it a date between the second half of the 5th and the first half of the 4th century BC. This period corresponds to the age of Chaonian superiority over the other Epirote tribes, and when, further inland in Molossian territory, the first fortified cities such as the acropolis at Cestrina, Tecmon and the Molossian capital, Pasaron, emerged (Dakaris 1964: 57). As for the polygonal style in Albania, it is usually encountered in one of three forms: in combination with the quadrangular; with one of the other styles of stone coursing; or, as an initial construction phase. The first and second styles were being used by the end of the 4th to the 3rd century BC, while the third could be earlier still (Scranton 1941: 45-68).

Sequentially the next style at Butrint, typified by the Lake Gate, is defined as 'coursed trapezoidal': blocks of different heights are placed in the same course, though in true trapezoidal style coursing does not exist. This style is classified by Scranton as 'irregular trapezoidal' when describing walls at Lissus, which are identical to the walls at Butrint. Considering them to be the work of Dionysius of Syracuse, Scranton dated the Lissus walls to the beginning of the 4th century BC. Elsewhere, at Teba Ethiotik, this style is dated to the end of the 4th century, probably on historical evidence. The same date is also confirmed at Lissus by evidence obtained by Prendi and Zheku from excavations, but Scranton still vacillates and dates Teba Ethiotik to the beginning of the 4th century BC, even though in both cases he noticed a tendency towards coursing (Prendi and Zheku 1972; Scranton 1941: 84). Coursed trapezoidal is also encountered in some other fortifications in Albania. At Phoenice, for example, this style is considered either as a second or third construction phase, whereas Hammond places the first phase of this fortified system, based on the large squared blocks, between the years 325-300 BC (Hammond 1967: 713-16; Ugolini 1937: 134).[3] Thus, the coursed trapezoidal of Phoenice cannot be earlier than the 3rd century BC. The coursed trapezoidal combined with the polygonal style is also present at Çuka e Ajtoit, as well as Lissus, but the combination of styles is more obvious at Çuka e Ajtoit, which exhibits Hellenistic features.

The combination of different styles, seen at Lissus between the late 4th and the 3rd centuries BC, is encountered at Antigoneia from the beginning of the 3rd century BC, and also at Lekel and Amantia (Budina 1972: 261). Hammond, having seen a large number of such fortifications in Epirus, came to the conclusion that 'The 3rd century saw almost every variety of style in the Greek world; it was an age of 'combination and elaboration' with ashlar style, pseudo-isodomic work and polygonal style. The coexistence of these styles makes it impossible to date a site precisely by the style of its masonry alone' (Hammond 1967: 713)· Scranton held similar views regarding Greek walls, whilst Wrede offered as a typical example of this period (3rd century BC) the later fortification

---

3 The wall in question descends towards the southern hillside and is connected to a quadrangular style wall made out of small blocks.

walls at Sounion, which he describes as having 'a strange combination of styles' (Wrede 1933: 59). Thus, dating is not entirely feasible for this period, neither for specific styles nor for where distinct styles coexist, to be able to clearly define the predominant practice of a particular period.

Accordingly, based on the style of construction, a date around the end of the 4th or the 3rd century BC should be attributed to Çuka e Ajtoit in spite of an earlier date having been ventured (Baçe 1979; Ceka 1976: 65; Islami 1975).[4] Establishing an accurate date for Çuka e Ajtoit is of great importance as it is the nearest fortification to Butrint, and the same construction techniques can be seen at both sites (Plate 3). Some architecturally compelling evidence, such as the large number of entrances, the character of the shifting wall line as well as the use of passageway entrances, indicates that Çuka e Ajtoit *should* date from around the end of 4th to the 3rd century BC, so there can be little justification in scepticism over the fact that the 'coursed trapezoidal' of Çuka e Ajtoit is of the same period as Butrint's (Winter 1971: 238-46). Meanwhile, excluding those parts confidently identified to specific construction phases, styles such as 'trapezoidal', 'polygonal' and 'quadrangular' were used in combination at Butrint too.

In forwarding a later date than that previously accepted for Butrint's 'coursed trapezoidal' walls, elements such as the consoles used in the gates are of some importance to the argument. Consoles were used in most of the gates in Butrint and are associated with the 'coursed trapezoidal' style of the Lake Gate and the North Gate, where, as we have already seen, the consoles are carefully and elaborately profiled. These features offer a certain degree of dating evidence, as they display a distinct development in their appearance. Profiled consoles appear later in the ancient fortifications, succeeding an earlier stage where protruding blocks were set progressively on top each other creating a false architrave. By the second half of the 4th century BC roughly profiled consoles were widely used in Selinunte and Heraclea near Latmos. Consoles closely comparable to those at Butrint can be found from the 3rd century BC onwards and frequently in the 2nd

---

4   Ceka (1976) dates the fortification of Çuka e Ajtoit to the middle of the 4th century BC by comparison with the Butrint fortifications: similarities in construction technique, and passageways entrance types, in combination with an absence of towers, are found at both sites. Islami (1975) thinks that the Çuka e Ajtoit fortifications can be dated to the late 5th to early 4th century BC. He cites the use of polygonal technique masonry and the type of gateways as evidence for this, techniques that have been used since prehistory. Baçe (1979) dates Çuka e Ajtoit earlier, to the late 6th to 5th centuries BC. His crucial argument for this date is the similarity of a passageway entrance to one at the fortified site of Pepel, south of Gjirokastra castle; however, he is not able to offer any convincing date for the latter. At Pepel there is a rectangular tower, an element that appears only relatively late in Albanian fortifications; furthermore, it seems likely that the passageway entrances date to the Hellenistic period.

century BC (Beschi 1968: 136). The 'long and sideways' arrangement used in wall construction, where at certain intervals stones are placed laterally within the wall, is a Hellenistic innovation (Winter 1971: 89). This technique is found only rarely in the 'coursed trapezoidal' walls at Butrint, as it is normally a feature of the isodomic and pseudo-isodomic styles. The majority of the architectural evidence regarding 'coursed trapezoidal' walls confirms that these walls cannot be dated earlier than the end of the 4th or the beginning of the 3rd century BC. The construction style at Butrint of massive trapezoidal blocks with roughly hammered surfaces (to lend the impression of strength), and the angled carving of corners in the walls was not effected to appear spectacular, as it was in the coursed polygonal or late polygonal styles, but to lend the walls an aged appearance. In light of historical events, particularly the flourishing of the city in the 3rd century BC and the importance it held for the expansionist foreign policy of King Pyrrhus, it would be logical to assign the main phase of defensive structures at Butrint to Pyrrhus. Pyrrhus was also the founder of Antigoneia to the northeast of Butrint, which has a large and impressive circuit of defensive walls.

The south wall of the fortified system that has the Tower Gate at its east end withstood numerous attacks over time. Much of the reconstruction work carried out in this section is plain to see and various construction techniques are evident. A 50 m long section stretches from the Tower Gate westwards to a square tower containing inscribed stone blocks (the so-called Tower of Inscriptions) that is dated to the middle of the 1st century BC, the same time that the wall to the east of the Tower Gate was rebuilt. The remainder of this wall was probably built by *c.* 230 BC, but it could also be dated to the second half of the 2nd century BC. The construction of the walls was driven either by the foundation of the Prasaebian *koine,* or by its later conversion into an independent state to protect itself from its neighbours' ambitions. The Dema Wall was one such defensive precaution undertaken by the Prasaebian tribe, so the wall in Butrint could also be dated after *c.* 232 BC. Other fortifications in the region such as Vagalat, Malathrea and the tower of Çuka could certainly be related to the foundation of the independent Prasaebian state, intimating a date for them of the second half of the 2nd century BC (Plate 3).

The 1st century BC – the 6th century AD: Roman and late antique structures

HISTORICAL CONTEXT

Butrint and its hinterland felt the colonial reach of Rome from an early time. The presence here of Italian traders from about 230 BC is attested by Polybius, while Cabanes states that the development of the protectorate after the first Illyrian-Roman war only reinforced existing trade relations (Cabanes 1974: 208). Cabanes also relates the presence of Roman names, such as Aulus, Marcus and Lucius in inscriptions in Butrint to the highly developed trade connection with the Italian peninsula, recording their incidence at Butrint, Phoenice and the port of Onchesmos as well as in the local population engaged in the cult of Asclepius and acts of manumission (Cabanes 1974).

According to Polybius, the number of Italian traders coming to the Butrint region was considerable. This topic is mentioned in his description of the Illyrian campaign in which Phoenice, the capital of Epirus, was captured (Polybius 2.8.2-3). However, even after the consolidation of the protectorate there are no sources to confirm the presence of a Roman garrison or extensive settling of Romans in Butrint as occurred, for instance, at Apollonia. In fact, recently discovered inscriptions indicate that Butrint and the Prasaebian *koine* maintained the same administration until at least 100 BC and this could well have continued until the first half of the 1st century BC as did the Thessalian *koine*, where silver coinage was being struck until the time of Caesar (Franke 1961: 219).

From the 1st century BC Roman settlement of Butrint became more prevalent as the city [may have] enjoyed the benefits of being a *municipium* from at least the middle of this century (Ugolini 1937: 89). The fertile soil around Butrint attracted the aristocracy of

Rome and by the middle of the 1st century BC the renowned landowner T. Pomponius Atticus, a very close friend of Cicero, held property near Butrint. By the later years of Cicero's life Butrint was settled with army veterans. Atticus was disturbed by the prospect of consolidated land being broken up for the colonists, but, despite his protests, a planned settlement proceeded. It is clear from the way in which the colonists were settled, the resistance of the local population and the perfect conditions for the development of agriculture, that Butrint was important both militarily and productively (Anamali 1981). The fortifications of the city served as a protected space for the colonists living in the outlying rural areas as well as for the Roman citizens living within the defended city.

Roman plans to fortify the area are documented from the time of the first colonists. The villa [previously attributed to] Pomponius Atticus, Amaltheon (Malathrea), is in fact a fortified building (Plate 3). However, the major settlement of colonists would have heightened the tensions between the Romans and the indigenous community. This situation is possibly the reason why Atticus was actually trying to prevent colonial settlement in Butrint: rather than being perturbed about his own private property, he was in reality fearful of potential conflict.

During the time of the civil wars Butrint was one of the main provisioning points for Caesar's forces. In his book *The Civil War* (3.16), Caesar mentions that 'Caesar, who had set out with one legion to recover the more distant communities and to expedite the food supply, which he was finding insufficient, was at Buthrotum.' Judging that the war against Pompey would be protracted and concerned about obtaining supplies from Italy Caesar sent two of his commanders to Epirus (probably to Butrint) to acquire wheat (Caesar *The Civil Wars* 3.42.3).

Augustus subsequently instigated a second colonial settlement in Butrint composed of civilian and military personnel. This foundation is attested by coin stamps with the inscription *Colonia Augusta Buthrotum*, on top of the fact that the colony was known by two different names, the other being *Colonia Julia Augusta Buthrotum* (Anamali 1981; Mustilli 1940: 6). By this time Butrint was of considerable importance in dominating the Straits of Corfu. The value of Butrint is also articulated by Cicero in a letter addressed to Atticus, in which he says that: 'Antium is to Rome what Butrint is to Corfu' (Cicero *Letters to Atticus* 4.8).

Despite the settling of Roman colonists at Butrint, Latin never became the official language, remaining only a spoken language, implying that the colonists did not assimilate the indigenous population. On the contrary, in the following centuries it was they who were assimilated by the native population (Anamali 1981).

The fertile lands around Butrint, the animal husbandry that benefited from excellent weather conditions, rich fishing and international trade all brought considerable prosperity to Butrint during the first centuries AD. For the first time in its history Butrint minted bronze coins during the reign of Augustus. In one example, the obverse of a coin carries a portrait of the emperor with the inscription *Buth(rotum) Augustus*, while on the reverse is an aqueduct and the inscription *T. Pompon Juli II vir* referring to the city's leading official (duumvir) (Ugolini 1942).

Firm evidence for the extension and development of the city is also provided by the remains of monuments dating from this period as well as the expansion of the city beyond its walls onto the Vrina Plain. A 3 km long aqueduct was constructed to supply the city with water, the building of which would have been highly expensive. It began at Xarra, famous for its abundance of water, crossed the Vrina Plain and the Vivari Channel and finally entered the city on its southeast side (Budina 1967: 145). The aqueduct was built during the reign of Augustus, most likely by the beginning of the 1st century AD. The great significance of this monument is plain from its depiction in the coinage of Butrint. At the same time the *scaena* of the theatre, which later underwent further reconstruction, was rebuilt.

There are also a considerable number of civic buildings from this period, including several public baths: one is located in the south part of the city close to the Vivari Channel; a second is close to the Tower Gate; and a third is near the Lion Gate. By the 1st century AD the shrine of Asclepius was constructed over the remains of an ancient shrine adjacent to the Theatre.

Around the 2nd century AD, a nymphaeum fed by water from the aqueduct was constructed close to the Tower Gate. The nymphaeum was faced with slabs of white marble while internally the basin was decorated with polychromatic marble. There is also the so-called gymnasium near to the Tower Gate, as well as a number of residential buildings of which the most attractive was a large villa with an atrium (built in the 2nd century AD) in the centre of the city close to the Theatre (Plate 4). These monuments typify the extensive building works that were executed in this period throughout the city and beyond the Vivari Channel on the Vrina Plain.

The continuity of life within the city until late antiquity is attested not only by archaeological material from excavations but also by numerous public and private buildings. The stratigraphic sequences of the 4th century AD demonstrate a progressive expansion of occupation, while the great number of coins implies a proportionate growth in trading activity (Lako 1977-78: 296). From the 3rd to the 4th century AD the city is variously referred to as Butaroton, Butarutan, Buthroto, Butroton, Buthrotum and Butharotum in the accounts of expeditions such as the

Itinerary of Antoninus (Cuntz 1990: 49, 76 and 324.5; 488.7; 499.1; Geographus Ravennas 1929-40: 94 and 4.8; 5.13; Miller 1988: 559-69).

In AD 458 Butrint is mentioned as an Episcopal centre at an ecclesiastical council of Epirus Vetus when the assembled bishops, including the bishop of Butrint, signed a letter forwarded to Emperor Leo I (AD 457-475) (Ugolini 1936: 319). By this time Butrint was governed from Nicopolis before subsequently falling under the control of Naupactus. In AD 516 Butrint is mentioned again as an Episcopal centre, while during the reign of the emperor Justinian the city is recorded by Hierocles (AD 535) under the name Butrytos among the 12 cities of Epirus Vetus (Hierocles *Synecdemus* 652.4; Ugolini 1936: 319). In this source other sites besides Butrint, such as Phoenice, Ankiasmos and Hadrianopolis were also recorded. These are the centres which controlled the main Chaonian territories: the Drino valley; the area around Delvina; and the Vrina Plain, with Hadrianopolis (Nepravishta) displacing Antigoneia, and Onchesmos (Ankiasmos) usurping Phoenice. However, with the appearance of the Prasaebians as an independent *koine* centred in the city, Butrint amplified its supremacy over Phoenice and Onchesmos. During the early Middle Ages it remained the most important site in the region at a time when Phoenice and Onchesmos were no longer mentioned in the Episcopal records of Leo VI (written *c*. 901-7 AD), whilst Hadrianopolis (Drinopoli) continued to dominate the Drino valley. Whilst sustaining its economic importance during late antiquity in comparison with other cities in the region, Butrint was periodically assaulted by barbarians, notably by Goths in 551 AD when Totila, sailing from Italy to Corfu, sacked the Epirote cities around Butrint.

During late antiquity intra-mural Butrint was the same size as in the Roman period, while individual monuments were built outside the walls. There is evidence of construction at this time everywhere in the region around Butrint, but the most important monuments, reflecting the contemporary prosperity of the city, are the Baptistery and two palaeochristian basilicas, one of which is situated on the acropolis and the other in the lower city (Plate 4).

The Baptistery, constructed around the middle of the 6th century AD, is one of the largest monuments of its type (Plate 33) (Ugolini 1934). It represents the highest architectural and artistic achievement in Butrint and provides evidence that at least until the middle of the 6th century AD the city remained sufficiently developed to create a monument of such architectural merit and with mosaics which display such a high degree of artistry (Plate 34). The Acropolis Basilica was built around the end of the 4th century AD and was also paved with mosaics, but one of the most important palaeochristian buildings, not just in Butrint, but in the whole of Albania, is the Great Basilica (Plate 35) by the Tower Gate (Meksi 1976; Ugolini 1942). This monument has three aisles (including a central nave), a rectangular narthex and a semicircular apse. It measures 30 x 16.75 m increasing to over 22 m wide across the transepts. The basilica was built at the beginning of the 6th century AD and its walls survive almost complete to their original height as it continued to be used until the first centuries of the early Middle Ages (Meksi 1976).

THE ROMAN DEFENSIVE WALLS

Judging from the surviving evidence, defensive constructions of the early Roman period occupied the highest part of the city, the 'upper city' (Plate 37). These constructions follow the southern line of the acropolis walls, occasionally built on bedrock, and include the wall descending from the northeast side of the acropolis to the Lake Gate. The northeast side was set apart from the ancient remains of the lower city, which occupy the steep slope on the south side of the acropolis, by a section extending down from the acropolis and joining the existing wall at the Tower Gate (Plate 37 F to M).

By following the traces of the early Roman constructions beginning at the south wall of the acropolis, at point A on Plate 37, a 7 m long wall section made from worked stones cut into regular rectangular blocks and set in even courses can be observed. The height of one course is 0.30 m, which is equal to one Roman foot, while the total height of the surviving wall is 4 m. The stones have worked, bulging, outer faces. They are carefully fitted together, apparently without bonding materials as in the earlier walls of the city, but on the interior the stones are fixed in a mortar matrix including small crushed stone. It appears that these walls were constructed by building two dry parallel walls in an isodomic order and then pouring a mortar core between them. Another section where the same technique is used, but where *spolia* have also clearly been used, survives close to the Lake Gate, beginning inside the gate and joining the south wall of the acropolis.

The wall construction technique described above is well known from Roman period buildings. It is a technique somewhere between *opus quadratum* and *opus cementum* as the core of the walls is formed in the manner of the latter technique. This method leant a wall better protection against the elements whilst being suitably aesthetic for important constructions. Thus, it was first employed in Rome and her territories from the end of the 2nd century BC, remaining in use until early in the reign of Augustus and, in exceptional examples, it persisted into the first centuries of the Empire up to the time of the Flavians (Lugli 1957: 314-5). Studies of cities along the Adriatic east coast have revealed that mortar was first used in fortification walls around the end of the 1st millennium BC while *opus quadratum* with mortar and prominent blocks (the latest examples including *spolia*), endures until Augustan times (Faber 1976). Based on this evidence, this technique most likely appeared in Butrint during the reigns of Caesar and Augustus, in other words during the first half of the 1st century BC until the beginning of the 1st century AD. This method, however, is not the only technique employed in Butrint's fortifications during the Roman era, in fact it is the least frequently occurring technique. Other techniques that account for the majority of the walls are described below to complete the picture of the fortified system during the Roman period.

Almost 25 m east of the section with quadrangular stones in the southern wall of the acropolis there are other traces of masonry from the Roman period (Plate 37 B), onto which the medieval acropolis wall was built. At this point stones are set in horizontal courses and bonded with quite thick mortar layers, over which small, almost square stones are irregularly placed. The use of these smaller stones in this fashion is related to *opus reticulatum*. This technique is clearly in evidence at the extension of the south wall of the acropolis (Plate 37 C). This wall was built onto the foundation of the ancient wall, which survives some 0.50 m wider than the later addition. The walls are constructed up to the considerable height of 6 m with stone slabs set in regular courses bonded with mortar layers up to 60-80 mm thick. The mortar is of good quality, mixed with small pebbles and has a reddish colour. The stones are usually around 0.10 m high although some are 0.40 m and occasionally 0.50 m high. It is clear that this wall is of the same type as the Theatre *scaena* and the aqueduct (both from the Augustan period), judging not only from the composition and colour of the mortar, but also from the technique of regularly coursed stone slabs.

Between points D and E (Plate 37) on the south wall of the acropolis there are small patches built in the *pseudo-reticulatum* technique within the predominant stone slab masonry. Occasionally tile fragments are also found between the stones, as well as some stones arranged in the shape of a fish spine (*opus spicatum*), another widely known Roman technique. This technique was used in some fortification systems in western Europe until the 11th century AD. The composition of the mortar is the same as that of the masonry with stone slabs, implying that these techniques were used simultaneously. Further east from these remains, at point F, another wall descends the hillside from the acropolis to southwest of the Tower Gate. Before heading downhill this wall adopts a rectangular form over which a medieval tower was later constructed. The part of the wall traversing the slope does not survive; however, from the extant remains it is clear that this wall was first constructed in the Roman period. It was built in the style of the walls described above with stone slabs placed horizontally and occasionally combined with the *pseudo-reticulatum* technique. Unique opportunity exists here to obtain information for the fortifications of this period, as the wall is preserved up to parapet level. The wall is 2.25 m wide, while the parapet adds a further 0.65 m.

Further east along the acropolis wall line, between points F and G (Plate 37), there are no surviving traces of walls dating from the Roman period. Evidence of Roman construction then reappears in the wall descending from the acropolis towards the Lake Gate. At the point where it physically joins the acropolis wall, however, it is clear that the descending wall is later than the acropolis wall. This evidence, coupled with the absence of Roman material in section F–G, implies that the Roman period wall followed a different line from the original wall, linking with the rest of the fortified system elsewhere and only after reconstruction work in the medieval period did the descending wall join the acropolis in its presently visible form.

At point G (Plate 37) there is a 7 m long section built using stone slabs. It is interrupted for a considerable distance by the medieval walls. The same technique reappears at point H (Plates 37-38), and continues up to the join with the *opus quadratum* wall. In this section the walls are preserved up to a height of 7-8 m. Important sections from the Roman period are also present in the north city wall along the lakeside. They are built directly on top of the ancient walls in the section between the Lake Gate and the Lion Gate (Plate 37 J-K, Plate 40). Along this section two quadrangular towers with wide faces project from the wall line. Both the walls and the towers are *c.* 10 m high.

At two points in the sides of the towers there is evidence of a technique not found elsewhere in the fortification system. The edges of the stones were deliberately obscured with mortar that was then incised by a trowel to create the illusion of rectangular stones set in regular courses (Plate 39). A small section of *opus reticulatum* built onto two or three courses of stone slabs in the walls between the towers indicates that they were part of the Roman period fortifications. The lower part of the wall was built with sub-rectangular blocks, roughly worked and ill fitting. The wall was rendered with a fine mortar skim that reveals the outline of the stones. In some places the mortar reaches the upper part of the wall where the stone slab courses begin. The same technique is also found in the Roman wall at point F (Plate 37), inferring that these walls were built around the same time. The superimposition of different construction techniques implies that they were practiced at the same time. So, in order to date these walls, it is necessary first to identify the latest construction techniques present.

Construction techniques

We will initially consider those walls built from stone slabs set in horizontal courses, which comprise the major part of the Roman walls at Butrint. In this technique, small rectangular blocks are placed in parallel courses, like *opus quadratum* in miniature but more correctly known as *opus vitatum*. Lugli highlights three types: plain; alternated with brick courses; and with brick courses (Lugli 1957: 63).

The plain type is encountered from the Augustan period onwards in circuit walls as well as in structures, such as theatres or amphitheatres, in cities in central Italy. *Opus vitatum* replaced o*pus reticulatum* as the latter was more complex to execute. During the Augustan period the plain type was generally preferred until the use of bricks became more widespread, as was the case in Butrint. However, the technique, either with or without bricks, remained in use until as late as the medieval period. It would be very helpful to be able to determine a *terminus ante quem*, not only for the *opus cementum* in the internal structure of these walls, but also for the *opus reticulatum* in the upper part of the walls between J-K (Plate 37) and to be able to identify the mortar composition and construction techniques that share common features with the *scaena* of the Theatre and the aqueduct. Although *opus reticulatum* was used from an earlier date than *opus vitatum*, the latter was only used for a short time and ceased to be used altogether from the time of the Antonines (AD 138-192) (Lugli 1957: 492).

The common features employed in the fortification system and the *scaena* of the Theatre are dated by Ugolini to the beginning of the Roman Empire (Ugolini 1935: 83). This early date is confirmed by the absence of bricks in the projecting arches of the *scaena*. Elsewhere in the *scaena* stones are placed in regular courses bonded with reddish mortar, as can also be seen in some sections in the south wall of the acropolis. As noted above, the technique of inscribing mortar into rectangular shapes around mortar-smeared irregular stones is also used for the fortification walls, and the two techniques could well be contemporary: mortar-obscured stones are also encountered in some later constructions, beginning with the shrine of Asclepius, whilst bricks are used in arches until late antiquity. Thus, it is not readily possible to distinguish phases in the construction techniques of the fortifications. However, considering them as a whole, together with the historical sources, the most likely time for their construction is between the second half of the 1st century BC and the first half of the 1st century AD.

The circuit wall of the lower city on the south side, which is interrupted by the Tower Gate, was retained in its original form during the Roman period and was reconstructed in places replicating the original technique. Excavations undertaken by Budina (1976-77) revealed a rectangular tower (Plate 41) in the wall line southwest of the Tower Gate. The outer measurements of the tower were 7 x 5 m and it was preserved to a height of three to four stone courses. The walls were two blocks wide, c. 0.45m high with intermittent blocks placed vertically to help strengthen the walls. Plumb lines were carved at the corners of the tower. Many of the blocks bear detailed inscriptions giving rise to the name of the 'Tower of Inscriptions'. The positioning of the inscribed stones either upside down or with the inscriptions hidden from view, coupled with the fact that many were cut down to achieve a uniform block height, implies that these stones were not *in situ*, but rather that they were brought in from elsewhere. [Following Budina's excavations the inscribed blocks were salvaged from the tower and assembled for display in a 'Wall of Inscriptions' (Plates 4 and 42)].

The inscriptions on the walls of the tower record manumissions dating from the 2nd to 1st centuries BC, so the construction date of this tower must be after this time. Its date can be further pinned down from the fact that the structure from which they were robbed would not have been destroyed immediately after the execution of the inscriptions. Furthermore, the inscriptions themselves have little relevance to the new tower as they were often damaged and placed upside-down. From the discussion above regarding the introduction of the use of mortar – from the time of Augustus – the period during which the tower may have been constructed narrows to between the time of Caesar and the early years of the reign of Augustus. The foundation of the inner wall of the fortifications at Lissus, which is of the same period, is closely comparable (Prendi and Zheku 1971; Zheku 1974).

The Tower of Inscriptions is an exception to the rule in the fortifications of Butrint in that mortar is not used even at this relatively late date. The maintenance of ancient local traditions in this structure can also be seen in the use of laterally placed blocks and the cutting of plumb lines at the corners of the tower, techniques which are similarly encountered in the wall at Lissus that was built at the time of Caesar. The wall running north-eastwards from the tower as far as the Tower Gate is also dated to the same period.

Whilst it is suggested that the Tower of Inscriptions and the wall heading towards the Tower Gate were contemporary, the wall itself cannot easily be investigated between the tower and the gateway due to soil and vegetation build up, although excavations have been carried out at its northeast end close to the Tower Gate. In the relatively short section over which it has been observed, the fortification wall is 3.20-3.40 m wide and has some technical similarities with the masonry of the Tower of Inscriptions, such as the use of angled stones and *spolia*.

The excavator at the Tower Gate, Kosta Lako, aimed to investigate the city's fortified system as well as to generate a more complete historical picture of life in this region from stratigraphic archaeological evidence (Lako 1981a). His report does not venture any new date for the wall, but concurs with Ugolini and his successors that the fortifications of Butrint had lost their original function by the time the Roman colony was established and were thereafter used primarily to support various buildings. The most interesting evidence gained from the excavation was that the fortification wall was used in various subsequent periods as an integral part of structures built against it, the layout of which was regularised in the earliest incidences. Square sockets were identified along the inner face of the fortification wall at a regular height and regular intervals to take the beams of a tiled roof.

A separate wall section, c. 0.60 m wide and parallel with the fortification wall was documented over a distance of about 25 m towards the west. Beyond this point the continuation of the wall remains unexplored. The wall is situated 5.60 m away from the fortification wall and has perpendicular walls built from it forming parts of small structures. The walls of these structures are made from limestone blocks that are lightly worked and laid in regular courses bonded with fine sandy lime mortar.

Lako's excavation was hampered by the perennially high groundwater table in Butrint. As a result, only evidence from the latest period of use of the structures was recovered: a thick stratified context c. 1.20 m deep, dated to the 2nd to 3rd centuries AD, although the structures themselves are unquestionably earlier. Lako considered this evidence as characteristic of normal urban activities in the mid Roman period. He asserted that the internal structures were not parts of the fortification system, although the inclusion of the beam sockets (which would have been impossible to insert later), argues that the fortification and the structure built against it at least belong to a single period of construction. It is feasible that the ancillary structures may have originally been used as a guardhouse. Again comparisons can be found at Lissus, where similar structures are placed in the same way and with the same purpose against the Caesarean-period inner wall face. The date of the arrangement in Butrint is probably a little later, but no later than Augustus.

Overall, from the assessment of the fortifications made so far one could conclude that during the early period of Roman occupation, and especially during the eras of Caesar and Augustus, a great deal of construction was undertaken at Butrint. The majority of this work took place during the reign of Augustus, when the second wave of colonists was settled in Butrint.

THE LATE ANTIQUE FORTIFICATIONS

The late antique fortifications at Butrint remain to be examined. As mentioned briefly above, the remains of exceptional monuments in the city are testament to the rapid growth Butrint experienced at this time. The physical extent of the city remained the same as in Roman times, although certain monuments were built outside the walls provided they were sufficiently safe from barbarian attacks. This construction phase is difficult to assess in that there are no distinct characteristic features (bar a single instance where a band of bricks is used) to help date the walls. This does not mean that we will repeat the mistakes of past scholars in confusing Roman or medieval masonry for late antique walls.

The results of the 2004 trench dug in the tower of the Western Defences (cf. Plate 43 P) have been of great help in defining the late antique phase. The Western Defences provided a barrier across the least protected side of the city. Tower P is rectangular in plan, measuring 7.60 m across its west face and projecting 6.20 m from the wall line to its rear. It is preserved to a height of 9 m. The thickness of the fortification wall is 1.80-1.90 m. Beneath a 70 mm thick burnt layer marking a catastrophic destruction event, late antique deposits containing many bricks and tiles have been dated to the 4th to 6th centuries AD. The late antique deposits also yielded a considerable number of coins indicating intense economic activity at this time. The tower is physically tied in to the defensive wall. Further to the south a second, U-shaped tower is included in the defences. From here the wall continues beneath a modern road towards the Vivari Channel, perhaps connecting with a currently isolated tower on the north bank of the channel. The presence of a U-shaped tower in the Western Defences, which is a typical arrangement of the 4th to early 5th century AD (as well as of a distinct 6th-century construction phase), may place the construction of the late antique walls in the 4th to 5th centuries AD.

The same construction technique used in the Western Defences, which includes few bricks, can be seen in the city wall close to the Triconch Palace where it turns through two right angles to include the palace within the fortifications. Walls of the same thickness (1.80 m), containing no bricks, also survive in other parts of the outer circuit, such as north of tower G at the edge of the Vivari Channel (Plate 43). However, the date of this wall remains uncertain.

Another section of wall, which from its construction techniques appears to date from late antiquity, still remains to be thoroughly examined. This is in the north wall of the fortifications near to the 'closing' wall that links the acropolis to the lake. It contains a band of three bricks courses, 8 m long and 2.40 m above the ground. The band is built on a thick mortar layer 70-80 mm deep. The bricks measure 440 x 400 x 45-55 mm and are divided by mortar layers 60-70 mm thick.

The construction technique of the brick band, in the number of courses, the ratio of the bricks to the mortar layers and the thickness of the mortar layer above, is immediately reminiscent of the second construction phase of the castle of Elbasan which is dated to the 6th century AD. In general, the ratio of the bricks to the mortar layers can be taken to indicate a construction date later rather than earlier in this period. Only limited restoration of the city's walls was required at this time as the Roman walls were still in good order. The west side of the city joining the Ksamil peninsula was the weakest part of the city, unprotected by the lake or the Vivari Channel, and the evidence from the tower excavation indicates that it was this point that was attacked and burnt. We do not know exactly when this event took place, though it could be equated with an assault by the Goths under Totila in AD 551. We know that Totila's forces, on their way from Italy to Corfu, ravaged the cities of Epirus, and this perhaps included Butrint.

By the 6th century AD, the reconstruction of the Dema Wall was one of the priorities for the defence of Butrint (Plate 3). At that time the most obvious threats to the city came from land-borne Avaro-Slavic invasions. Accordingly, late antique restorations can be seen in the section ascending the hill from the lake and in a rectangular tower. There are also other rebuilt sections on the hilltop close to the Monastery of Saint George. It is not possible to ascertain precisely the line of the late antique wall as little survives of the ancient substructure upon which it was built. It can be said, though, that the wall was constructed with rough stones bonded by lime mortar mixed with sand and gravel. Stones in the façade were set in regular courses, levelled by rectangular slabs of stones, while ancient blocks were reused in the foundations. Between the courses small pieces of crushed stones were inserted, a technique reminiscent of the Justinianic wall at Byllis.

The fortification had small rectangular towers of which only one is preserved to a height of almost 2 m. It is located on the west side of the Monastery on the hilltop plateau. It projects 2 m from the wall line and is 2.70 m wide. The internal space is small (1 x 1 m), while the wall thickness is 0.70-1.00 m. The south and the east walls are the thickest, as they have flat ground in front of them, while the west wall of the tower is thinner. The construction period of this fortification cannot be established based on its technical features alone. During the late antique period mortar often contained pieces of brick, pebbles and gravel up to 30-40 mm in diameter. Similar material is documented at a great number of late antique castles in Albania, such as at the castles of Bellova, Gjonomadhi, Zvezda, in the third phase of Trajani castle at Korça, in a second construction phase at the castle of Elbasan, as well as at some castles near to the Via Egnatia such as the castle of Qafa, the castle on the King's Rock and the castle of Braja. In these latter castles the technique appears as a second or third construction phase during late antiquity (Ceka 1974: 72, 77, 79-80).

Barrier walls, such as at Zvezda near Korça, are known from the prehistoric period onwards. The example at Butrint is early, but there are also late antique constructions of this sort such as at Porto Romano near Durrës. These structures were erected to protect cities from unexpected attack as well as to allow for the engagement of as many people as possible in the defence of the city. Proposals for this type of construction are often recorded from the 6th century AD. Thus, Anonymous of Byzantium suggested the construction of the outer fortified walls was intended to ensure that the citizens could play a role in defending the city. Procopius, the historian of Justinian I, meanwhile, also recommended that such fortifications be built not only in cities but in the areas surrounding them. Since not all cities were situated in suitable terrain for such barrier walls, the same effect was achieved by constructing large outer circuit walls within which there was sufficient room to take in the rural population.

The 7th–15th centuries AD: medieval structures

HISTORICAL CONTEXT

Butrint seems to have been amongst those cities that either stood firm against or avoided the barbarian incursions and, despite varying fortunes including the darkest period of its history in the 7th and 8th centuries AD, occupation persisted from antiquity through to the medieval period. This is evident not only from surviving material culture and the maintenance of the city's name, but also from historical sources.

The anonymous supplement of Hierocles that includes a mention of Butrint is thought to refer to the period after the 6th century AD (Krumbacher 1897, vol 2: 417). By the end of the 9th century AD Saint Elias the Younger is named as resident in Butrint (Rossi Taibbi 1962: 42, 116, 153). In a bishops' list from the time of Leo VI (AD 886-912), which was probably written in c. AD 901-907, Butrint is mentioned as a bishopric, dependent on Naupactus, since the metropolis of Nicopolis no longer existed (Ugolini 1936: 323). By the beginning of the 10th century AD, Arsenius bishop of Corfu (AD 876-953), records the valuable fish and mussel resources of Butrint as well as the fertility of the land around it. From the time of the reigns of Simeon and Peter (AD 927-968) until the death of Samuel (AD 1014), Epirus was under Bulgarian political and ecclesiastical dominion. The dioceses formerly dependent on Naupactus now came under the main diocese of Ohrid, but according to a list in the Athenian codex, by the time of John Tzimisces (AD 969-976), Butrint was apparently a diocese governed by Nicopolis. This implies that the Bulgarian occupation did not extend to the Ionian coastline close to Butrint, even though this region must have been continually threatened by the Bulgarians. The Slavic place names in the area around Butrint also bear testimony to this foreign presence.

A diploma of the Byzantine emperor Basil II in AD 1020 suggests indirectly that Butrint was indeed under the rule of Ohrid in the time of Czar Peter (AD 927-968) (AA.VV. 1962: doc. 9). The diploma defines Butrint and Himara as two of the bishoprics of southern Albania, entitling them to 12 clerics and 12 parishes each, meaning that they were only modest dioceses. Dependency on Ohrid was merely ecclesiastical, a situation that remained even after the fall of the Bulgarian monarchy when Durrës also came under ecclesiastical control from Ohrid. The dependency was not long lived, though, as the descendants of Basil II did not enact his decrees and the dioceses of Epirus returned to the control of their previous metropolis (Ugolini 1936: 325).

By the end of the 11th century AD the Byzantine Empire was under threat from invasion by Norman forces. In May AD 1081, a Norman army under Bohemund, son of Guiscard, captured Vlora, Kanina and Jerikon, and reached Butrint where they joined Guiscard. The oldest major work in French literature, the *Song of Roland*, provides evidence for the participation of a garrison from Butrint in the war against the Normans. The story of Baligant, Emir of Babylon, in the *Song* (considered to be a later addition), was inspired by the first confrontation between the Normans and Alexius Comnenus that took place near Butrint (Gregoire and de Keyser 1939: 269). A number of other fortified cities in Albania, such as Kanina, Oricum and Byllis, are mentioned as also having confronted the Normans (Luka 1967: 139). In the tale of Baligant a character named Basil Mesopotam (from Mesopotam near Delvina) appears leading the multi-ethnic Byzantine troops, suggesting that the confrontation with the Normans in this area was undertaken by local people (Luka 1967: 129). It seems plausible then, that near Butrint this feudal lord, Basil Mesopotam, can be associated with the castle of the same name. Elements of the walls and of a number of square towers of Mesopotam castle survive around the Church of Shën Koll, which, according to Ducellier, was later converted into a fortified building before becoming ruinous by the 11th century AD (Ducellier 1981: 43; Meksi 1972).

Guiscard captured Butrint and pitched camp nearby. Thereafter a naval battle between the Norman and Venetian fleets took place off Butrint, with the Venetians emerging emphatically victorious. By AD 1084 Butrint served once again as a base for Norman incursions inland. From as early as the 9th century AD, Butrint is mentioned as being involved in various important events and the city's large population is testified by the remains of monuments such as the Great Basilica, reconstructed in the 11th century AD, the scale of which would have been too grand for a small city (Meksi 1976). The Great Basilica may also have been reconstructed around the end of the 9th century AD, when a

The 7th–15th centuries AD: medieval structures

wholesale rebuilding of the outer city wall took place, indicating the importance of the city at this time.

By the middle of the 12th century AD Butrint served as an important army and naval base. In AD 1149 the Byzantine Emperor Manuel Comnenus stationed his fleet in Butrint with a view to capturing Corfu which was then under the rule of Roger, King of Naples and Sicily (Morosini 1687: 111). In AD 1185 the Arab traveller Al-Idriz mentioned Butrint as a small, populated city with a market.

The period from the 10th to the beginning of the 12th century AD is characterized by intense economic activity in Butrint. This is indicated by the discovery of a large number of medieval coins in a small area of the city; these include examples of Constantine Porphyrogenitus (AD 944-959), Nicephorus II Phocas (AD 963-969) and John Tzimisces (AD 969-976), as well as coins of Alexius I Comnenus (AD 1081-1118). What is most striking is their proliferation during the 10th century AD. Before the 10th century AD early medieval coinage began and ended with the coins of Phocas (AD 602-610) (Lako 1981b: 127-9). This interruption, or diminution, in the distribution of coins is documented not only in Butrint, but across the whole of the Byzantine Empire. This was the result of a general economic and political crisis that befell the Byzantine Empire during the 7th and 8th centuries AD.

In the aftermath of the annihilation of the Byzantine Empire by the Fourth Crusade in AD 1204, an independent state known later as the Despotate of Epirus was founded under Michael I Angelus Comnenus with its capital at Arta. The arrival of western and Venetian nobility in the east during the crusades brought western influence to the architecture of eastern cities, although Butrint, as it was incorporated into the Despotate of Epirus in AD 1205, maintained its Byzantine architectural influences. It was not until the 14th and 15th centuries AD that western features began to emerge in the architecture of the city. In AD 1258 Butrint came under the dominion of the king of Sicily Manfred Hohenstafen, having been given to his daughter Helena as a marriage present by the Despot Michael II of Epirus (Thalloczy, Jiricek and Sufflay 1913, vol 1: 71 no 245). After the time of Michael II, Butrint was controlled by the Byzantine Emperor Michael VIII Paleologus who stationed a large garrison there in AD 1274 (Hopf 1870: 300).

At the time Butrint served as a military post for Paleologus, the city was also a base for piracy organized by the Byzantine state. In May AD 1277 two pirates from Butrint ('people of Byzantium') hijacked a Venetian ship loaded with cereals at Spinaric and steered it into Butrint where the grain was off-loaded (Hrabak 1970: 29). Similarly, in June of the same year, two Venetian traders shipping leather from

Spinaric to Durrës, plus 11 fully armed ships at Anaea and one at Butrint, were captured by the same pirates. All of these vessels wound up in the hands of the well-known pirate Jan de la Kavo from Karija (Ducellier 1981: 249).

A year later, in AD 1278, Butrint was taken by Nicephorus, the Despot of Epirus. However, at the beginning of the following year he handed over Butrint, together with the castle of Sopot (Borsh), to Charles I Angevin King of Naples under a previous agreement struck between the two. On April 7th, during the handover period, the Angevins sent supplies of food and weapons to Butrint. The occupation of Butrint was of great strategic importance to the Angevins who intended to use it, along with Durrës, Vlora and Corfu, as one of their bases for planned invasions of the Balkans. To enable this, Charles I made alliances with Byzantine enemies, notably with Nicephorus. On August 13th AD 1294 Charles II of Anjou made his son Philip, the prince of Taranto, ruler of Corfu, Butrint and all the Angevin territories in Epirus (Hopf 1870: 337).

From AD 1279 until AD 1386 Butrint remained under the control of the Angevin princes with just two intermissions (Ugolini 1936: 327). The first of these took place in AD 1306 when the Despot Thomas, in negotiation with Philip of Taranto, exchanged Butrint for two other cities; the second break occurred between AD 1313 and AD 1331. From the time of the Angevin occupation, Butrint was firmly associated with Corfu and remained as its satellite on the mainland. This relationship is clearly alluded to in Angevin documents, where 'the castle of Butrint in Corfu' is mentioned. Whereas some other cities on the Ionian coast, such as Sopot and Himara, were also under the control of Corfu, Vlora was directly governed from Naples. Only Butrint and Corfu were given to Philip of Taranto in AD 1294 (Miller 1908: 249). Ducellier notes that after AD 1285 Angevin Albania was limited to the fortress of Butrint and the territory around it, the exact borders of which are not readily defined (Ducellier 1981: 273 (Reg. Ang. 1268 0, f. mm5)).

By AD 1320 Butrint was under the command of Nicola Orsini, Count of Cefalonia, who offered the Venetians Butrint's profitable fishing in exchange for help against the Byzantine Emperor, but was refused (Ducellier 1981:326). Before the Venetians took over, from AD 1380 to AD 1382, Butrint suffered a brief occupation by the Navarese. In AD 1382 Butrint was well populated, as is clearly demonstrated by the numerous privileges given to the inhabitants by Charles III of Durrës (Barone 1887: 27; Ugolini 1936: 327-8).

In AD 1386 Butrint finally fell to the Venetians who were interested in Butrint's strategic position in relation to Corfu, her rich fisheries and the famously fertile land in the area. In May AD 1394 the construction of the castle of Butrint was ordered and it was emphasized that there were plenty of cereal crops in the local territories (Hrabak 1970: 51; Valentini 1967-75: vol 2, doc 245, 15.V.1934). The Venetian government in Corfu was authorized to buy and distribute grain from Epirus that was only to be shipped to Venice herself (Hrabak 1970: 52). It is possible that the Venetians also exported grain from Butrint during the first decades of the 15th century AD until the capture of Vlora by the Turks (Hrabak 1970: 51). Although the city diminished in size from the end of the 14th century AD, her location opposite Corfu meant that Butrint retained strategic value during the 15th century AD when Corfu was considered by the Venetians as 'the gateway of Italy' (Monti n.d.: 320).

These, then, were the main historical events affecting Butrint during the medieval period. There is evidence of these events in the city's building activity and in its fortifications, which will be analyzed in the following pages.

Firstly, the city was encircled by an outer wall along the shores of Lake Butrint and the Vivari Channel (Plate 43). Defence of the less well-protected approach from the isthmus was reinforced by double walls 15-20 m apart. The inner wall had rectangular towers and a U-shaped tower, built in late antiquity (see above), but reused in the 9th century AD. The inner wall ended with a tower close to the shore of the Vivari Channel, while the outer wall had no towers and ended at the U-shaped tower, creating a medieval *proteichisma*.

At the highest point of the ancient city – the acropolis – an elliptical area 280 m long x 70 m wide [87 m at its widest point] was enclosed with fortification walls. From its eastern side a section of wall descended the hillside northeast to the Lake Gate where it joined the line of the ancient wall. On the west edge of the acropolis, another important defensive point, a castle was built with a tower or keep inside its enclosure walls. This complex fortified system was constructed over a long period, as can be illustrated by the numerous construction techniques visible and by the different forms and dimensions of the towers in the circuits.

THE OUTER FORTIFIED WALL CIRCUIT

The northern part of the fortifications followed the line of the ancient walls, while to the south, east and west it was built from ground level during late antiquity and the medieval period, thereby doubling the enclosed area of the city from the time when the original walls were built. Now at its fullest extent, the fortified area covered 16 ha and the total length of the medieval walls, including the inner sections, was *c.* 2,500 m.

Beginning the description of the outer medieval fortifications heading west from the Lake Gate, it can be noticed that ancient and Roman walls predominate as far

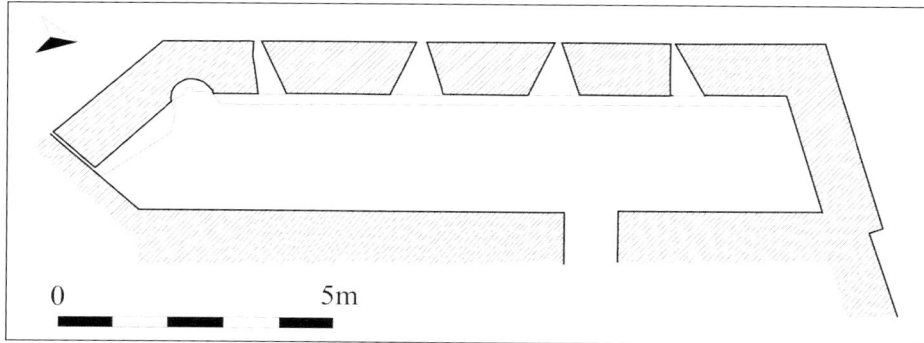

Fig. 9 Guard house (cf. Plate 43 point 3)

as the Lion Gate. Beyond the north side of the city walls it is worth mentioning a medieval section located at a point before the wall links with a section descending towards the lake (Plate 43 point 1). Here the medieval wall is built straight on to ancient blocks and is composed of stones of different sizes with horizontal brick fragments within the vertical lines of mortar. The same technique is also seen where the section descending from the hill towards the lake joins the main wall as well as where the wall turns south (Plate 43 point 2). In both instances ancient blocks were reused.

Immediately after the turn in the wall at point 2, there is a section where the stones are set irregularly and bonded in strong mortar with no bricks present. Further on there is an 8 m high section made from both stones and irregular brick courses. It is similar to some of the walls and towers in the outer walls on the south side and with the second phase of the wall between the castle and lake. A long trapezoidal structure was later built onto the outer face of the wall at this juncture (Fig. 9, Plate 43 point 3, Plate 44). This structure is 13.50 m long x 2.50 m wide with walls 1.10 m thick. The structure has four firing loops and a garderobe (Plate 45). Two of the loops are slanted, angled towards the southwest, while the other two are

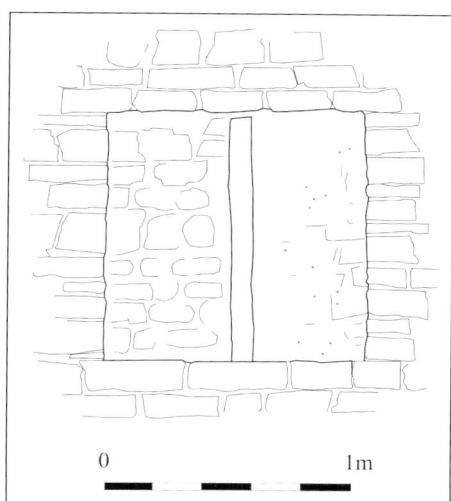

Fig 10 Guard house, elevation of firing loop

The 7th–15th centuries AD: medieval structures

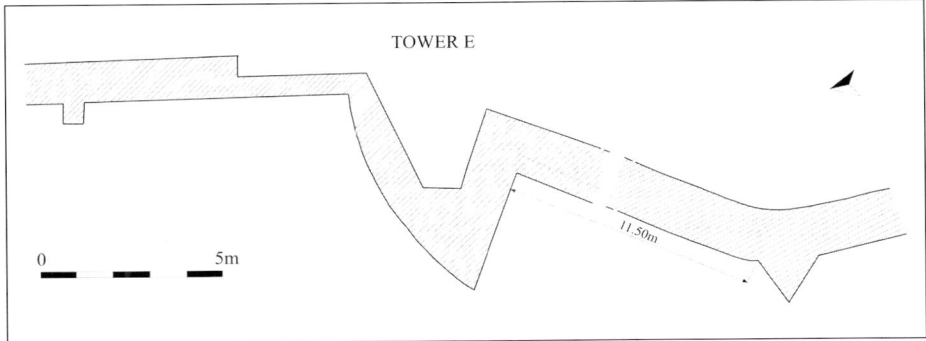

Fig 11 Tower E and adjacent wall

plain triangular in form (Fig. 10, Plate 46). The loops are 1 m high and narrowing from 1.05 m wide on the interior to just 0.10 m wide at the exterior. The garderobe is set into the wall and has a sloping channel that empties on the outside of the wall. It is clear that this structure was used as a guard block. The walls are made with stones bonded with mortar including brick fragments, a technique which resembles the third phase of the 'closing' wall linking the castle with the lake.

After a break in the standing walls, a 90 m long section descending to the south includes a triangular tower and regularly spaced pilasters (Fig. 11, Plate 43 E). The construction technique is uniform, hence it can be assumed that it was all built at the same time. The wall is 1.50 m wide and 5 m high in the best-preserved part; where traces of the battlements survive it is up to 7 m high. The reinforcing pilasters, or buttresses, have rectangular (Plate 47) and triangular sections. The former are 0.80 m long and project 0.60 m from the wall, while the latter are 1.90 m long at their base and project 1.50 m from the wall. South of the triangular tower there are three firing loops in the wall, 3.40 m above ground level. The loops are triangular, 0.85m wide on the inside, 0.10 m on the outside and 0.45 m high. Timber scaffold holes, of which a couple can be seen only in tower E, are not found in the walls.

Tower E (Plates 43 and 48) has an irregular triangular shape: one of the faces is shorter and perpendicular with the wall, while the other, which forms an obtuse angle at the junction with the wall, is curved. The walls of the tower are 1.20 m thick. On the inside the tower has a straight façade, which completes an irregular trapezoidal plan. In both the curtain wall and the tower there are many reused ancient blocks and stacks of bricks or tiles set horizontally on top of each other. The upper parts of the wall are made with smaller stones but using the same technique. There are short, interrupted courses of bricks, but the north wall of tower E is crossed by an uninterrupted band of two brick courses. Along the whole length of the wall the mortar is of good quality and is thickened with coarse sand and pebbles.

Just beyond the base of the hill to the south, all traces of this wall disappear. The flat terrain at the base of the acropolis hill is protected by two parallel walls [the Western Defences] that run towards the Vivari Channel. It is difficult to determine which of these walls is the one that joins with the triangular tower E, but it is more likely that the tower was linked to the outer line of the parallel walls; the south side of the city, meanwhile, was probably unfortified at this point in time. Two square towers are still preserved, along with a U-shaped tower, on the inner wall of the fortification (cf. Plate 4). The inner wall continues towards the Vivari Channel, ending with another tower, and at some point probably met the channel-side wall that enclosed the southeast part of the city. The outer, medieval, wall forms a *proteichisma*. It does not run as far south as the inner wall, but stops shortly after the U-shaped tower and turns a right angle before joining a spur from the south wall of the tower. In the northern part of the *proteichisma*, in front of tower P, there is a shallow rectangular projection in the wall in the shape of a tower, but with a broad façade.

Tower P, preserved to a height of about 9 m, holds the history of this section of the defences (Plate 43). The 2004 excavations here showed that the tower and the walls were built during late antiquity. It subsequently burnt down and was rebuilt in the 9th century AD. The 9th century AD tower floor was paved with reused bricks from the Roman and late antique periods. Finewares from the 9th century AD were found *in situ* on the floor. The 9th century AD tower was covered with a timber and tile roof and timber floor joists. The tower burnt down again and was never rebuilt. The fire appears to have started in the roof and then consumed the lower wooden structures. The latest coins are of the 11th century AD, suggesting that the tower may have been razed during the Norman invasion at the end of the 11th century AD.

Tracing the line of the wall alongside the Vivari Channel, one first encounters an 18th century tower constructed in the Venetian style. Being much later, the Venetian Tower has no bearing on the appearance of the medieval fortification circuits; indeed, it was constructed when this stretch of wall no longer existed. Further on, some 50 m east of the Venetian Tower, a Roman building is incorporated within the width of the defensive wall.

The wall subsequently turns 90° towards the Vivari Channel, where it is 1.85 m wide and made from stones and occasional brick pieces, reminiscent of the late antique wall by tower P. The shift in direction of the wall line gives the impression

The 7th–15th centuries AD: medieval structures

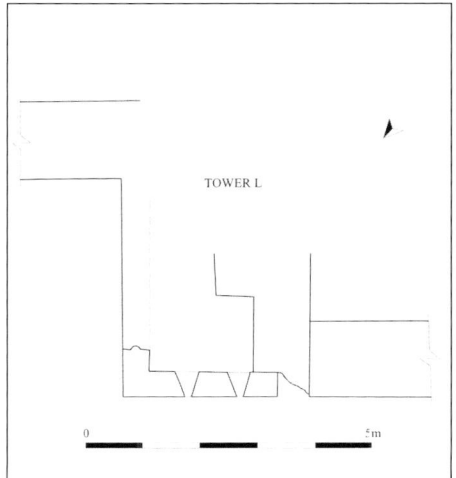

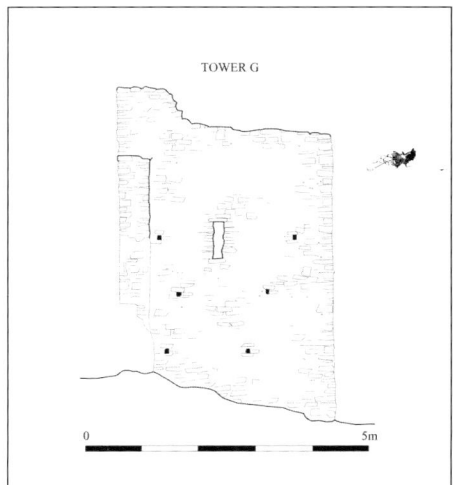

Fig 12 Tower L, plan showing construction phases

Fig 13 Tower G, south-facing elevation

that it intentionally included the Roman Triconch Palace within the circuit. East of the Triconch Palace a square tower (L) (Fig. 12, Plate 43) occupies another small dogleg in the defensive line: the west side of Tower L overlooks the exterior of the fortification whilst its east side is on the inside of the wall. The unusual manner in which the walls are attached to the tower betray the fact that the staggered arrangement is not a unitary design. The southern façade of tower L stands to c. 8 m high and has two firing loops with rectangular sections at first floor level (Plate 49). The loops are 0.50 m wide on the inside, constricting to 0.15 m on the outside and are 0.65-0.70 m high (Plate 50).

The wall to the west of Tower L is contemporary with the tower whilst that to the east is somewhat later, though it is not possible to accurately date either section. The tower itself is the result of two distinct construction phases (built prior to the wall to the east), in which the walls of the second phase are 0.60 m thicker than their predecessors. The construction technique visible in tower L is distinct from that of towers P (see above) and G (see below). There are a number of brick fragments inserted in its walls, some irregularly, but for the most part horizontally. There are also brick fragments in the vertical lines of mortar. This appearance is similar to some of the reconstruction work in the south wall of the acropolis as well as in the wall descending towards the Lake Gate.

Northeast from tower L a corner of what was tower J (Plates 43 and 51) survives to a height of 5 m. Its construction technique is similar to that of tower G. Some

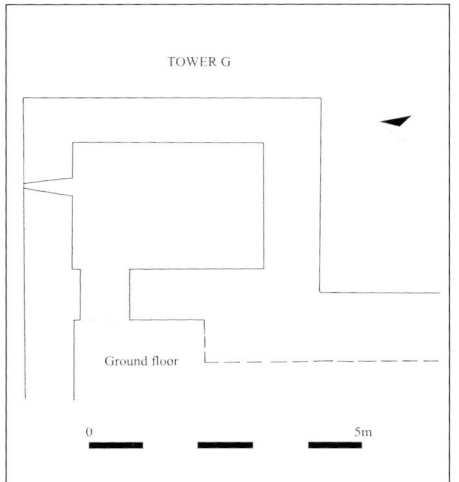
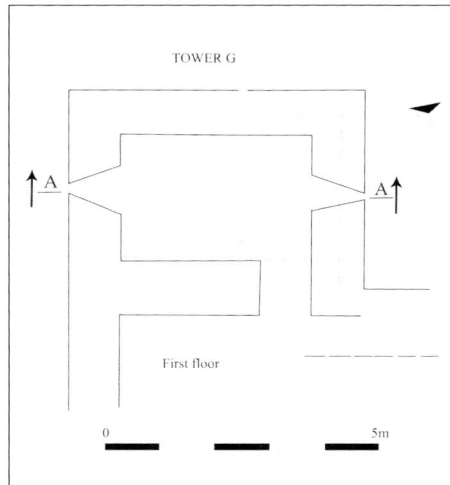

Fig 14 Tower G, ground floor   Fig 15 Tower G, first floor

45 m beyond tower J the fortification turns again through another right-angled dogleg where an earlier Byzantine construction is incorporated within it.[5] After the turn, the wall follows the channel bank northwards, where the wall-walk and crenellations survive in part (Plate 52).

Eighty-five metres further on, a well-preserved square tower (G) occupies the angle of another turn in the wall line (Fig. 13 and Plate 43 G, Plate 53). Tower G is built over two storeys: the first storey is filled almost to the level of the top of its entrance. It measures 3.40 x 2.30 m inside and the walls are 1 m thick (Figs 14-15). The two storeys did not communicate internally, but were separated by timber floors supported on wooden beams carried in wall sockets measuring 0.20 x 0.20 m. The first storey was accessible through an arched doorway in the west side (Plate 55). The entrance to the upper storey is 0.87 m wide, framed by a wooden lintel and it connected to the city wall-walk. The upper floor consisted of a single space with a single firing loop piercing each of the three exterior-facing tower walls. The loops are triangular in plan, 0.70 m high, with an inner width of 0.55-0.85 m reducing to 0.12 m on the outside. The firing loops, like the entrance, were covered by wooden lintels, remains of which can still be clearly seen (Plate 54). The upper floor is crowned by a cylindrical vault springing from the north and south tower walls (Fig. 16). Above the vault are the remains of a firing platform

5   Editor's note: the 'Byzantine construction' is a large and elaborate house with a cross-vaulted cellar and living quarters on the first floor. It is a design typical of major town houses throughout the Venetian empire and is more generally recognised as dating from the 15th or 16th century.

The 7th–15th centuries AD: medieval structures

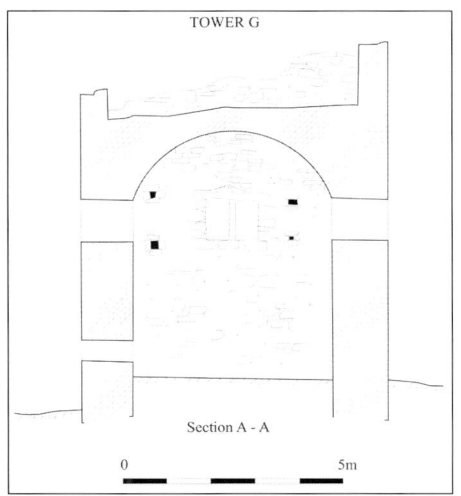

Fig 16 Tower G, section A-A

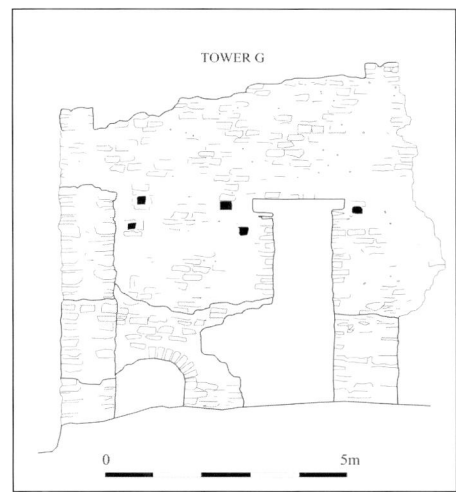

Fig 17 Tower G, west-facing elevation

with vestigial traces of battlements (Fig. 17). The tower walls are constructed from roughly shaped stones and occasional irregular brick fragments, but with no horizontal brick courses. The tower is of a later date than the first phase of the Water Gate (see below), but is from the same period as the walls at point 3 (see above) on the west side of the outer circuit.

At tower G the wall takes a sequence of right angled turns to frame a gateway set 10-14 m back from the main circuit line. At the gateway, known as the Water Gate (Plate 56), a wall-walk is carried above a structure containing pilasters and brick-framed relieving arches. This section of wall survives for 23 m, interrupted by an entrance 1.40 m wide and 1.85 m high. The entrance is framed by an arch of bricks that measure 0.35 m long. The thickness of the mortar between the bricks is 60 mm, while the bricks themselves are only 30-40 mm thick. Two distinct periods of construction can be identified in this section of the fortifications (Fig. 18). The brick-arched gate belongs to the second phase; the entrance was formerly larger and remains of the original arch are preserved in the north side of the outer façade (Fig. 19, Plate 57). The second phase also saw the blocking-in of some of the relieving arches beneath the wall-walk. This can be seen most graphically in a half-open arch at the south end of the gateway. The arches, along with the construction style, which uses interrupted brick courses and irregularly inserted brick fragments, are reminiscent of the technique used in the nearby Great Basilica (in the second phase of the flanking walls of the nave).

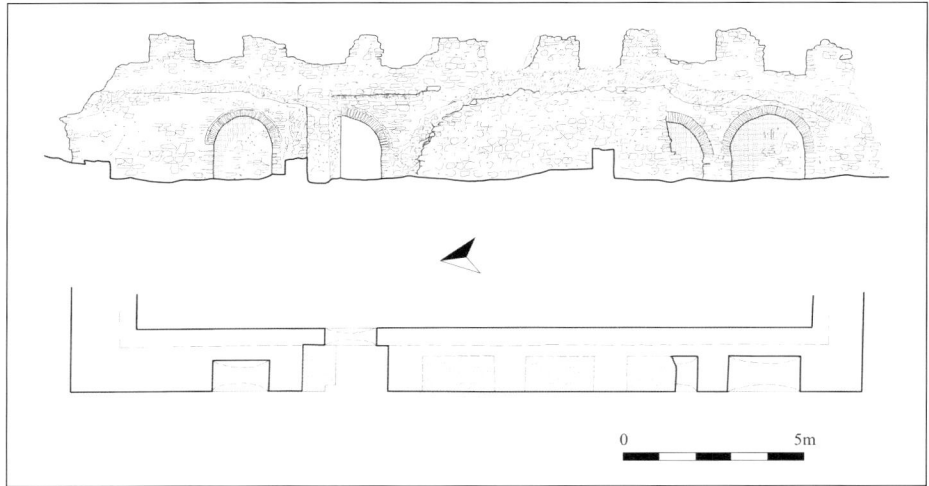

Fig 18 The Water Gate, west-facing elevation and plan showing construction phases

Beyond the Water Gate the style of construction changes around point 6 to include larger, coursed stones with no bricks, evocative of the walls in the Western Defences (Plate 43 P). A small postern gate is located at point 5. Further on, at point 4, there is another small, arch-covered gate, while on the inside of the wall there is a large stone structure, possibly the foundations of steps leading to the wall-walk. At this point the fortification wall is 1.80 m thick and the battlements are 0.60 m thick. The wall-walk is only 1.50 m above ground level.

From point 4 as far as the Lake Gate the fortifications are limited to low sections topped with embattled parapets. It is extremely difficult to investigate the construction technique of these walls, especially close to the Lake Gate, as they are adjacent to the waters of the lake and are entirely overgrown.

THE WALL LINKING THE ACROPOLIS AND THE LAKE SHORE
A wall was constructed from the northwest of the acropolis fortifications across the strip of land reaching down to the lake shore (cf. Plates 43 and 58), closing off and controlling access to the north side of the city from the isthmus. This medieval period construction was undertaken to ensure that the natural protection afforded by Lake Butrint and the Vivari Channel on three sides of the city was reinforced and as effective as possible. Thus, instead of gaining rapid access to the principal defences, any would-be attacks from the land would first have to negotiate an outer barrier. The same principle can be seen in the construction of the Dema Wall near Ksamil.

The 7th–15th centuries AD: medieval structures

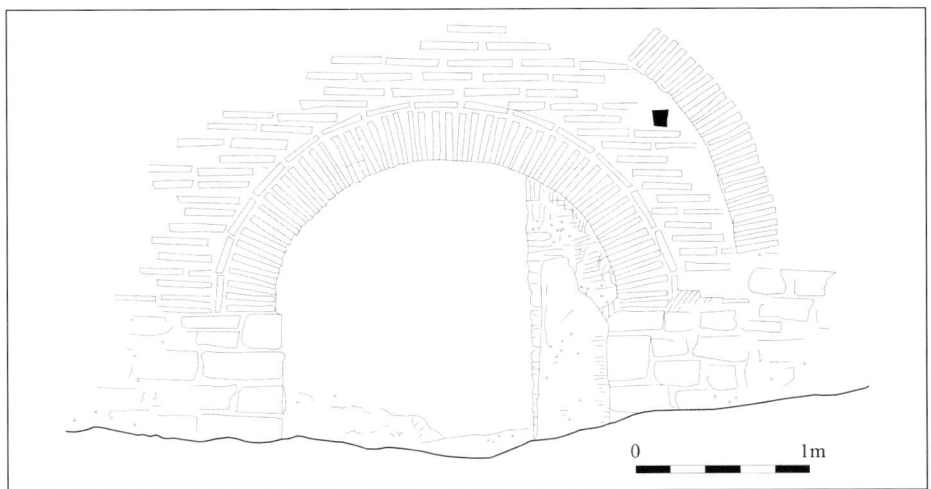

Fig 19 The Water Gate, east-facing elevation showing construction phases

The wall measures 55 m long between the acropolis circuit and the lake shore, and in places is preserved up to battlements level, 10 m high. At the point where it abuts the acropolis enceinte the new 'closing' wall is clearly the later construction. Three phases of construction or rebuilding are visible in the wall itself, which therefore indicates at least four separate periods of refortification in the medieval period. The majority of the remains of the 'closing' wall that survive today comprise the first recognisable construction phase and stretch over a distance of some 35 m downhill from the acropolis defences.

In part, the 'closing' wall is founded upon an ancient construction of rectangular and trapezoidal blocks. The medieval masonry built over these blocks is reminiscent of the technique used in the tower and triangular bastion of the western part of the acropolis circuit where re-used blocks are bonded with mortar and horizontal brick fragments are inserted in vertical lines between the blocks (Plate 43 D). The first phase of the 'closing' wall employs the same technique, although ancient blocks are not included as *spolia*. Discontinuous horizontal courses of brick can also be seen and occasionally brick fragments are placed vertically (Plate 59). In these examples we are witnessing a long lived construction technique as well as two separate construction phases, where the earliest is that re-using ancient stone blocks.

The first phase of the 'closing' wall linking the acropolis with the lake is punctuated by an entrance that was later blocked in. The entrance measures 1.20 m wide and is adorned with a brick arch. The provision of an entrance in the 'closing' wall implies that the wall not only protected the north part of the acropolis fortifications, but also served as a convenient exit route in times of danger. A short distance north of the entrance the remains of a staircase to access the battlements wall-walk still survive (Plate 61).

Elements of the second identifiable phase of construction are also preserved up to the height of the battlements, remains of which indicate a width of 0.45 m. The second phase wall, measuring 1.46 m wide, is some 0.30 m narrower than the first phase construction. The remains of a rectangular tower survive up to 5 m high, extending 2.80 m out from the line of the curtain wall and measuring 4.40 m across (Plate 60). The construction technique is markedly different from that of the first phase, with more abundant use of bricks in the wall face. The bricks are set in interrupted horizontal courses or placed irregularly within horizontal bands of mortar. There is no evidence, in the shape of putlog holes, for the use of timber scaffolding. The second phase wall bears resemblance to some of the towers and sections of wall in the south part of the outer, channel-side circuit as well as to some parts of the walls in the southern extent of the acropolis circuit.

Some reconstruction of the wall became necessary and evidence of a third phase of building can be seen close to the lake shore: a stretch of wall is attached to the outside of the second phase rectangular tower. This wall is 1.25 m wide and is preserved up to the level of the battlements, which were originally 0.60 m wide. Again, the construction technique differs from the preceding phases. Abundant bricks and brick fragments are inserted irregularly within the lines of mortar, with most set vertically.

THE FORTIFICATIONS OF THE ACROPOLIS

Two phases of medieval period walls were recorded in the north extent of the acropolis fortifications where there was evidence neither for prehistoric or other earlier substructures, nor for re-used material. The earlier of these two phases (Plate 62) runs for a length of 50 m from the west end. This section includes two bastions, one triangular the other rectangular, above which is a massive rectangular tower of the later phase of construction (Plate 43 D). These architectural elements replicate features of the western outwork fore-guarding the acropolis wall circuit (Plate 43 E). Whilst the outwork is but a short distance from the acropolis defences and may appear to be part of the same fortification campaign, the construction technique of the two is not the same. The outwork uses generally short neat bands of brick between stone courses and small stacks of brick between blocks. Brick and tile are used abundantly in the outer face of the acropolis wall section, but the pieces are placed irregularly. Occasionally the bricks are placed perpendicular and rarely in pairs. Elsewhere, brick is entirely absent from the wall, such as in the north face of the triangular tower. Though the military architecture is the same in both examples, it is considered that the acropolis section is a later build and illustrates a decline in the stylistic devices used in the facing of the western outwork.

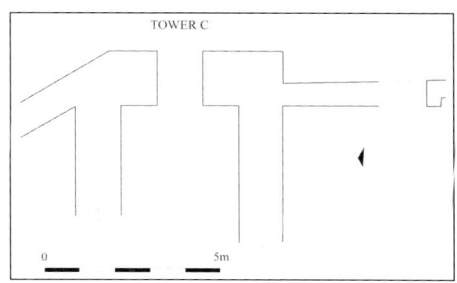

Fig 20 Tower C, plan

Further east, the construction style of the north wall of the acropolis circuit takes on a completely different character. The four massive rectangular towers and the curtain wall of this section are constructed in the same style (Plate 43 A-D). Neat, squared stones are set in irregular courses bonded with strong mortar containing coarse inclusions (Plate 63). Brick is rarely used in the facing and there is evidence of square timber scaffold (putlog) holes (Plate 64).

Tower D measures 6.70 m wide and projects 4.50 m outwards from the wall. The tower masonry is 1.35 m thick. Between towers D and C a demolished wall, 0.80 m wide, projects out obliquely from beneath the medieval masonry. This could possibly be the remains of the earlier phase medieval wall that would have been completely destroyed prior to reconstruction.[6]

Tower C is preserved to c. 5 m high. It is rectangular in plan (Fig. 20), 6.10 m wide, but its side walls are not well preserved and could not be measured accurately. One of these projects c. 4 m from the circuit wall, while the other extends 3.50 m. The thickness of the tower walls is 1.35 m, the same as tower D. Only traces of an entrance 1.20 m wide remain, but a second entrance, allowing access up to the acropolis, is preserved in the circuit wall on the west side of the tower. The gate through the circuit wall is capped by a large stone lintel with smooth faces supported on two consoles, one of which is broken. The consoles are reminiscent of those used at the Lake Gate, but for that they are more rudimentary. Some fragments of brick and tile are included in the side walls of tower C, but this alone does not call into question its chronology regarding the acropolis circuit wall and other towers on the north side.

6 Editor's note: the oblique remains described are those of a much earlier wall, dating almost certainly from the Roman period.

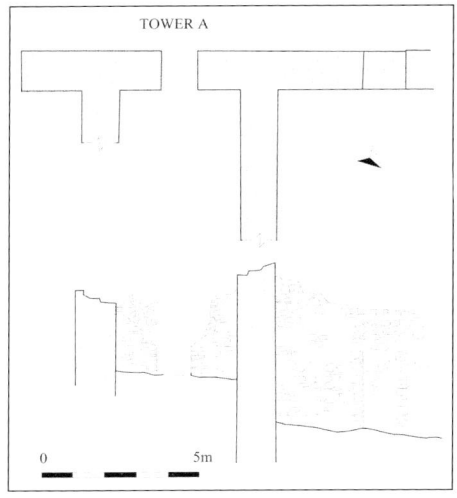

Fig 21 Tower A, plan and northeast-facing elevation, and adjacent blocked gate

Tower B (Plate 65) is preserved up to 8 m high, projects 5.30 m from the wall and is 6.80 m wide. It is in a derelict condition and the core of both side walls is exposed. There is evidence for timber scaffold poles within the core.

Tower A also stands up to 8 m high and is the final tower on the acropolis circuit that belongs to the second medieval phase of building. The side walls of the tower are not wholly preserved, but measure 1.35 m wide, equivalent to the width of the fortification wall at this point (Fig. 21). Traces of the enceinte battlements can be discerned close by, which were originally 0.60 m wide. An entrance, 1.10 m wide, is situated in the centre of the tower's rear wall, though the top of the gateway has collapsed. This entrance would have allowed access into the tower at first floor level and it is possible that it was the only entrance into the tower, as the terrain within the enceinte was higher than that outside. As at tower C, a gate leading to the acropolis is situated in the fortification circuit wall to the west of tower A. The entrance is 1.30 m wide and is crowned with a plain brick arch. This entrance was later blocked with mortared masonry blocks and rubble.

Beyond tower A the acropolis fortification wall curves towards the south. About 20 m from the tower a separate section of wall (described below) descends the hillside to join the channel-side circuit by the Lake Gate. The construction style typified by the rectangular towers is maintained a little further as the wall swings south-westwards, but it is subsequently superseded by another distinct wall type characterized by frequent use of irregularly placed tile and brick fragments. Indeed, ceramic fragments are widely used along the whole of the southern flank of the acropolis enceinte. Another characteristic of the defensive wall on the south face of the acropolis is that it is built on top of earlier walls, some prehistoric, but especially Roman structures.

At point F two phases of construction are apparent, one Roman, the other, above it, medieval (Plate 43 F). In the medieval phase wall, groups of horizontal brick fragments are often set in the vertical lines of mortar between stones. This technique bears resemblance to the first phase of construction in the wall linking the acropolis with the lake to the northwest. In this latter wall, only at ground level, the face of a triangular tower built using the same technique can just be discerned.

Triangular projections can also be observed in the southern wall of the acropolis circuit around point F. This section of wall was replaced at some point by a straight retaining wall 1.50 m wide that includes randomly placed brick pieces with some examples set vertically. Just to the east of the retaining wall is an entrance to the acropolis measuring 1.50 x 2.50 m. The entrance (Plate 66) was originally topped with a stone lintel and a wooden ceiling, traces of which can be seen where the timber has decayed away. Beyond the entrance to the east, the wall takes a sharp bend following the hilltop contour and thereby forms a broad triangular projection. At the apex of the triangle a shallow semicircular tower was constructed (Plate 43 O). Tower O displays considerable use of brick fragments, though rarely are they set vertically (Plate 67). This technique is similar to the second phase of the wall linking the acropolis to the lake shore as well as with some walls and towers of the outer, channel-side circuit protecting the lower city. The mortar used in the tower is good quality with many pebble inclusions.

Between tower O and the wall that descends the acropolis hill down to the Lake Gate, the southern acropolis enceinte exhibits a number of variations in construction style. The technique employing bricks gives way to a style without bricks, which has more in common with the wall with the rectangular towers on the north side. This, in turn, continues to a point where the wall face is offset *c.* 1 m. Here, a new face has been applied to the circuit wall; use of brick fragments then resumes sporadically as far as the wall connecting to the channel-side circuit at the Lake Gate.

The wall between the acropolis and the Lake Gate

A section of wall zigzags down the hill from the northeast of the acropolis circuit towards the Lake Gate, linking the northern lines of the fortification system and thereby defining the so-called upper city (Plate 43). This section of wall preserves some important remains from the Roman period (see above), especially close to the Lake Gate, and the medieval wall is frequently built upon demolished Roman wall tops. At the top of the hill the wall abuts, and is therefore later than, the second phase acropolis wall of the north side with rectangular towers. It is considered to be contemporary with the wall on the southern flank. Bands of brick and tile are used as stylistic devices interrupting stone courses. Elsewhere, brick fragments are

Fig 22 Southeast-facing elevation of gate in the wall linking the acropolis with the Lake Gate

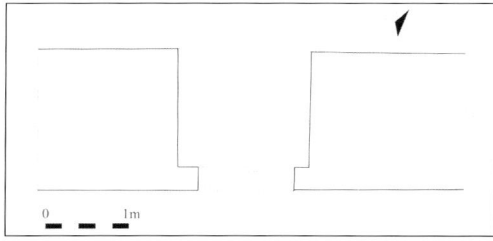

Fig 23 Plan of gate in the wall linking the acropolis with the Lake Gate

commonly set within horizontal mortar layers and occasionally within vertical sections between stones. In some places bricks are placed vertically or in groups surrounding stones.

Around its midpoint the wall is pierced by an arched entrance (Figs 22-23). It measures 1.20 m wide and 2 m high. Large re-used stone blocks form its sides while its arch, 0.23 m thick, is worked out in rectangular stones decoratively interspersed by tiles. The thin tiles measure 0.22 x 0.18 x 0.03 m. The top of the arch is surrounded by a 20 mm thick band of tiles. The depth of the entrance/thickness of the wall is 2.05 m, and around this point the wall stands to between 7-8 m high. The construction style of the entrance bears close comparison with the outer entrance of the fortified courtyard at Berat castle, constructed by Michael I Comnenus Doucas in c. 1205 (Baçe 1971).

The Acropolis Castle

The castle comprises a sub-square keep built into the north wall of an irregular five-sided enclosure (Plate 4). This form is similar to the tower built by Theodorus Comnenus Doucas in 1225 at Durrës castle, which, according to Léon Heuzey was provided with a residence and an inner courtyard (Heuzey and Daumet 1876: 349-92). At Butrint, the keep would have served as the living quarters of the castle commander. The castle is built on the highest and most readily defended point of Butrint (Plate 68), from where much of the city's outer walls, along with the less

The 7th–15th centuries AD: medieval structures

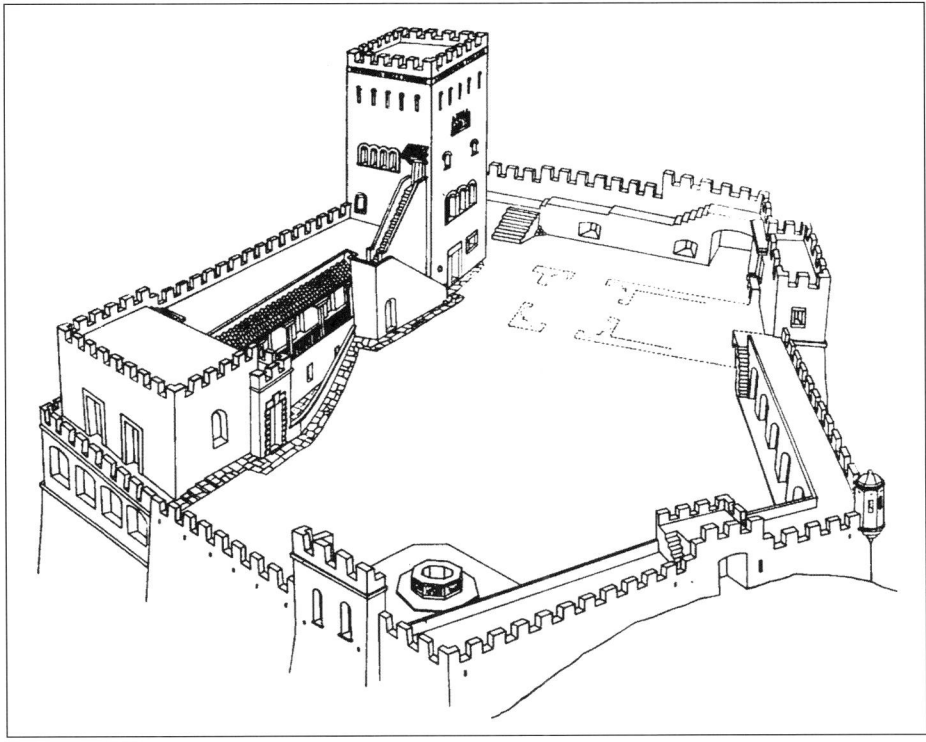

Fig 24 The Acropolis Castle, reconstruction by the Italian archaeological mission (Instituti i Arkeologjisë)

naturally protected parts of the city, could be observed. The keep directly overlooks much of the northern acropolis fortification wall as well as the gated entrances to the acropolis.

It is not possible to make a detailed description of the medieval castle as the entire complex was reconstructed by the Italian archaeological mission without recording sufficient information about the original remains. The restoration works were carried out following stylistic criteria based on interpretations by the architect Carlo Ceschi during c.1933-34 (Fig. 24). Only the ground plan and certain of the better-preserved sections of wall were retained from the original layout (Ugolini 1937: 54). Thus, the present appearance of the Acropolis Castle and its keep are more the product of the restorers' imagination than historical accuracy. Because of these circumstances it is not feasible to ascertain the earliest parts of the castle complex with a great degree of certainty. However, some elements in the north face of the keep and the eastern enclosure wall (Plate 69), where the main entrance to the castle is situated, do resemble the construction technique of the latest parts of the southern acropolis wall and of the lower city wall along the Vivari Channel. Part of the enclosure wall is preserved to wall-walk level, including elements of the parapets (Plate 70). The construction style of these features is comparable with that of the lower part of the keep. Some of the cannon on display (Plate 71) were brought to Butrint from Gjirokastra.

On the southwest side of the acropolis, an additional wall was built over the ancient city wall as a revetment to relieve downward pressure caused by the building of the castle. It was built with a slope from top to bottom and included two relieving arches that show it was designed as a retaining wall.[7] The arches, built with stone blocks interspersed with tiles, are very similar to the entrance in the wall linking the acropolis with the Lake Gate and are much like constructions of the Epirus Despotate period at Berat. Indeed, both here and at Berat castle, the number of tiles set between the stones switches randomly between two and three.

Construction techniques

The medieval fortifications of Butrint clearly occupied a far greater area than those of earlier periods. The number of phases of construction and re-building indicates the importance of the city during medieval times, a fact that is not evident from the fragmentary written sources alone. However, the problems in correlating so many phases that are similar, or have only small variations in style make it difficult to determine an absolute chronology and, therefore, the significance of any given structure at any particular time. That said, it is at least possible to offer some preliminary conclusions about the medieval fortifications from observations of different techniques of wall construction, based on their physical relationships and with reference to masonry styles seen elsewhere.

The earliest general style visible in medieval Butrint is characterized by the use of brick and tile placed horizontally within vertical lines of mortar. This style, with small variations, persisted over a long period. Within these variants it seems likely that the earliest form is where large stones or reclaimed ancient blocks are used. Constructions in this style are found directly above the remains of ancient walls, as in the north side of the outer wall circuit. Amongst the best examples of this technique can be seen at the junction where the 'closing' wall

---

7   Editor's note: the sloping retaining wall is entirely a reconstruction by the Italian mission styled on Despotate period masonry. The Italian photographic archive contains images that appear to show one or more original terraced retaining walls *in situ* at this point rather than a single battered wall.

runs up from the northern lake shore to meet the acropolis enceinte and in the western outwork at tower E.

In order to determine the exact date and longevity of this style, we need to look outside Butrint to examples in better dated monuments and to see where this technique features in the relative chronology of other structures. Elements of the castle of Berat and nearby church of Shën Koll at Perondi are architecturally close and are most likely the work of the same mason. Shën Koll contains three principal construction phases (Meksi 1973: 32-33). The first phase, dated to the 10th century, is worked out in the same fashion as Butrint's tower E, with horizontal brick courses and brick pieces 'stacked' horizontally in vertical lines of mortar. The second phase, dated to the beginning of the 13th century, consists of stone masonry interrupted by bands of four to five courses of bricks, while the third phase, dated to between the 13th to 14th centuries, is constructed in *cloisonné* style (Meksi 1973: 32-33).

At Berat, meanwhile, those walls built with re-used ancient blocks and containing brick fragments within vertical mortar layers, are placed directly on top of ancient walls (where they are present). This is repeated at the main entrance, in the inner courtyard and the courtyard tower. A brick monogram of Michael I Comnenus Doucas is set on one side of the entrance vault to the courtyard and upon this evidence the courtyard and adjacent tower are dated to the beginning of the 13th century (around 1205) (Baçe 1971: 43-58). However, this date is subject to debate, as parts of the courtyard and entrance were reconstructed during the time of Michael I and the construction technique of the upper elements of the courtyard walls is entirely different from that of the lower parts. The fortifications of Michael I are represented by walls with small, faced stones. The majority of walls and towers at Berat castle include brick bands of four to five courses, in the same fashion as the second construction phase of the church at Perondi.

With these comparisons in mind, the period at the end of the 12th to the beginning of the 13th century can be regarded as a *terminus ante quem* for the first building phase at Berat castle. As such, it is possible that the courtyard here could have originally been built by the 11th century, or even earlier, as was Perondi church. An earlier date may be intimated by the style of certain walls in the medieval castle of Lissus. Here, as at Butrint and Berat, there are examples of mortared re-used blocks with bricks and stones in the vertical mortar lines built over ancient walls. A castle at Lissus is mentioned as early as the 9th century, which pushes back this distinctive building style to even earlier times.

The same technique can still be seen today in the walls and towers of Skopje Fortress in Macedonia. The Fortress was rebuilt in the 10th to 11th centuries, an event that may coincide with Skopje becoming the centre for a Byzantine military Theme (11th to 12th centuries) (Deroko 1971: 15-16). Considering the style of construction in these structures, however, they could well be earlier. Both Skopje and Berat are equipped with three forms of tower: rectangular, polygonal and triangular, but before discussing these architectural elements, it is worth pursuing the extent and dating of the early style masonry elsewhere, and in other types of monument.

A similar technique can be seen at the church of Shën Ilia at Buhal near Permet. Because of the use of perpendicular and herringbone brickwork this masonry belongs to a later period, perhaps the second half of the 11th to the first half of the 12th century (Meksi 1975a: 81). Another church, closer to Butrint, on a low hill above the Pavllas River at Çiflik, is dated later still, to the end of the 13th century by the coincidence of *cloisonné* type masonry alongside the early style (Meksi 1977: 76). A number of religious monuments in the territories of northwest Greece, such as Epirus, Acarnania and Aetolia, also display the early style. Like Butrint, these regions belonged to the same Byzantine Theme of Nicopolis from the early medieval period. Numerous examples can be found in churches of the 8th to 9th centuries, the early and later 10th century and through to the 13th century (e.g. at Vlacherna near Arta) (Vokotopullo 1975: 23, 185, 188, 191-2, 196).

In Albania, the early style was largely supplanted by *cloisonné* style masonry during the 13th century, a fashion that continued in popular use throughout the following century. Nevertheless, the early style persisted here and there in conjunction with *cloisonné*, such as at Berat and Apollonia, where the lower elements of walls are built with the early technique and the upper parts with *cloisonné*. The two can be seen in combination in one of the towers of the castle of Durrës, constructed by the end of the 15th century under Venetian dominion. This argues not only for a continuation of a strong local tradition, but also for the construction of the fortifications at Durrës by local craftsmen under Venetian control. The same can be observed in certain Angevin period constructions in the city.

Returning to Butrint, we can consider the chronology of the architectural elements of the walls near tower E in relation to other medieval constructions in Albania. At the outset, it is worth establishing that almost all of the triangular towers of Berat belong to the first medieval phase of construction and some small triangular towers at Kanina (with a ground plan 2.60 m wide and sides 1.90 m long, which correlates with those at Butrint) also date from the earlier medieval period. The small towers are constructed from re-used ancient blocks and include brick pieces within the mortar. The early phase walls at Kanina are, as at Butrint, placed directly on top of more ancient walls (Baçe 1974: 34-35). Apollon Baçe dates the walls to the 10th and 11th centuries based on the recorded involvement of Kanina in the Norman-Byzantine wars (Baçe 1974: 41). This interpretation is supported by excavated material from one of the city gates, beside the triangular walls, which revealed that the earliest medieval phase dated to the 10th century (Baçe 1974: 34-35). The medieval castle at Shurdhah, built by the end of the 12th or the beginning of the 13th century, offers good parallels to Butrint in its triangular towers, the absence of putlog holes in the curtain walls as well as firing loops through the thickness of the walls (Spahiu and Komata 1974).

Relying only on construction styles and other architectural elements, the first phase of the medieval fortifications of Butrint could be dated to within a wide time span, from between the second half of the 8th until the 13th century. However, bearing in mind that the early phase is succeeded by four later construction phases, the last of which is not later than the period when Butrint was taken into the Despotate of Epirus, it is suggested that the most likely time when these defensive structures were built was during the second half of the 9th or the 10th century, with war between Byzantium and Bulgaria as the backdrop.

The acropolis walls with triangular projections are of similar date to tower E and the adjacent section of wall. The first medieval phase of the acropolis south wall can not be later than the second construction phase of the Great Basilica, which is dated to the 9th to 11th centuries. In the 9th century, the wall of the Western Defences with the rectangular and U-shaped towers was reconstructed (and walls in the channel-side circuit may have been repaired around the same time). A second wall, without towers, ran parallel to the towered wall of the Western Defences, forming a *proteichisma*. In tandem, these walls protected the city on its least naturally defended side, the approach from the isthmus. The combination of *proteichisma*, which itself is very rare in the early Middle Ages, with the triangular bastions appears to be an isolated example in the Byzantine Empire. The prosperous reign of Emperor John I Tzimisces (AD 969-976) might provide an appropriate context for their construction.

The fortifications of this period seem more comprehensive than those of Roman and later Roman times, with the whole city fully enclosed within natural and man-made defences. Taken together, the surviving evidence gives us a picture of how the city's fortifications appeared during the two first centuries of the early medieval period. Thus, we may conclude that, prior to the Norman incursions of the late 11th century, Butrint was indeed fortified, in spite of Dusselier's assertion that Butrint: "....can not really be considered a fortified place" (Ducellier 1981: 43). The city's rich economy during the 9th to 11th centuries suggests further that Butrint was not merely functioning as a religious centre at this time.

The second phase wall on the north side of the acropolis with the rectangular towers A-D was constructed at a point after the first medieval phase (9th to 11th centuries) and before the 13th century. The most likely time of this construction is, therefore, during the 12th century, a period when Butrint was an important base in the Ionian for the Byzantine Empire. In this phase of (re-)fortification, works were also undertaken on the southern and eastern sections of the lower city walls along the Vivari Channel.

This set of constructions was duly followed by another two distinctive phases of building, where brick and tile fragments were widely used. To summarise, in the first of these phases, brick fragments were predominantly placed horizontally within vertical mortar lines; examples can be seen at point F and tower O on the acropolis, in the earliest phase of the 'closing' wall descending to the lake on the north side of the enceinte and in tower L on the lower city circuit. In the second phase, brick fragments were more often set irregularly, though horizontal placement is still much in evidence. This phase can be identified in the wall linking the acropolis to the Lake Gate, in the second phase of construction, in the northwest wall descending to the lake as well as in the rectangular towers G and J on the lower circuit.

Unable to arrive at a precise typology for these constructions at the time of the field survey, as their style is not sufficiently differentiated to be dated by comparison elsewhere, reliance has been placed upon historical context, relative chronology and some architectural elements to propose a date of the 13th to 14th centuries for this period of fortification. Certainly, during the relatively turbulent times of the Despotate of Epirus it seems logical that there would have been important fortification works at Butrint as well as reconstructions of the earlier period defences.

Previously in this discussion attention was drawn to the similarity of the gate in the wall linking the acropolis to the Lake Gate with the entranceway of the fortified castle courtyard at Berat. Moreover, the rectangular towers with firing loops on Butrint's southern lower wall circuit also bear certain architectural resemblances to the rectangular towers built at Berat during the time of Michael I Comnenus Doucas. It is also worth mentioning here that the firing loops in both towers and walls are not designed for musketry, confirming that they were constructed prior to the appearance of artillery. This conclusion is supported by the fact that the walls are relatively thin and vertical, as at tower L, measuring only 0.60 m wide. It is considered that the following group of constructions at Butrint belong to the same period: the south wall of the acropolis; the acropolis to Lake Gate wall; a section of the acropolis to the lake 'closing' wall; towers and wall rebuilds on the lower city circuit; refortification along the north side of the city; and the keep (and probably the entire Acropolis Castle complex) in the southwest corner of the acropolis enclosure.

Some historical sources, though not wholly reliable, are of assistance in dating the construction of the Acropolis Castle. Andrea Marmora, writing in *The History of Corfu* in 1672, mentions an inscription in the walls of Butrint of the name of the Despot Michael II, who, whilst living on Corfu, built new walls at Durrës, fortified Arta, and built various churches as well as the castle at Butrint (Marmora 1672: 211). The same claim that the castle was built by Michael II, in 1236, is made by Donald Nicol, but with no reference to the source of this information (Nicol 1957: 132). However, there are no surviving monograms or inscriptions of Michael II in the walls of Butrint. The attribution is certainly credible though, as the construction activity of the Epirote Despots throughout Albania is well testified. It was quite common for them to inscribe their names on buildings such as the monogram of Michael I at Berat castle and the inscription of his son Theodorus in one of the towers of Durrës castle. Furthermore, the construction style used by Theodorus at Durrës is entirely similar to the castle at Butrint. Finally, it is clear that within the relative chronology established here for the walls of Butrint that the construction technique used in the Acropolis Castle falls into the period of the Epirus Despotate and from this period Butrint is referred to as a 'castle' (*castrum*), especially in Angevin texts (Ducellier 1981: 13).

The third construction phase of the 'closing' wall linking the acropolis with the lake is of a later period. The most likely time for its construction is the period between the second half of the 13th to the end of the 14th century.

The final construction work at the Acropolis Castle relates to the period of Venetian occupation and, to judge from the type of firing loops built, the work was probably undertaken in the 15th century. The loops were inserted in existing walls of different construction periods; actual defensive structures from the Venetian period at Butrint are themselves rare. An order for the construction of a castle at Butrint was given in May 1394, but there is no surviving detail regarding the commencement of this work and it seems likely that it was either postponed for lack of funds or otherwise unaccomplished. Moreover, it is uncertain as to whether the order refers to the acropolis or the Triangular Fortress on the south bank of the Vivari Channel.

The late 13th–19th centuries: Venetian and Ottoman structures

HISTORICAL CONTEXT

From the time Butrint was captured by the Angevins around the end of the 13th century, and more so a century later after it was seized by the Venetians, the importance of the city as a fortified centre began to fade, though its value as a strategic base remained. Within a very short time its economic value exceeded even its strategic worth. This phenomenon began around the end of the 15th century when it became apparent that the castle could not withstand the aggressive intent of the Ottoman Empire. For this reason expenditure on the city's defences was relatively small and confined to protecting Butrint's valuable fisheries.

The 15th to 16th centuries were a stressful period for the Venetian authorities at Corfu in regard to Butrint. For example, following the capture of Constantinople in 1453, Mehmet II sent an army of 10,000 soldiers to assault Butrint in 1454, though this met with no success (Marmora 1672: 261). A short time later, as a result of deteriorating relations between Naples and Venice, Butrint was captured in 1456 by Simon Zenevisi, who made an alliance with Alfonso the Magnanimous, king of Naples, as previously had Skenderbeg and other Albanian princes. After the capture of the area around Gjirokastra by Ottoman Turks, Zenevisi still possessed a castle at Cape Vagenetia, 4 km southwest of Konispol, opposite Corfu. We know that in *c.* 1454 this castle was occupied by Aragonese foot-soldiers well equipped with weaponry and munitions, which caused considerable embarrassment to the Venetian governor on Corfu (Marinesco 1923: 88-93, 114-5). Eight years later, in *c.* 1462, 2,000 soldiers were sent from Corfu to the Ksamil peninsula to head off an Ottoman army advancing on Butrint. This occurred prior to the more general breakdown of the

Venetian–Ottoman peace and the Ottoman invasion of Corinth in 1463 (Marmora 1672: 268). By the end of the 15th century the Venetians were anxious for both Butrint and Corfu as a large Ottoman force assembled nearby on the mainland. Butrint was considered as the key to Corfu, but in 1498 it was reported that the castle at Butrint was in very poor condition with only 12 guards stationed there (Zamputi 1967, vol 4: doc. 265).

In February the following year it appears that construction works were undertaken around the castle and city of Butrint, as well as at Parga, but work only proceeded so far due to a lack of finance (Zamputi 1967, vol 4: doc. 265). Inevitably, Butrint came once more under threat from the Ottomans in c. 1501, when a great number of soldiers were gathered around Saranda and Butrint with the aim of pressurising Italy into helping the king of Naples (Zamputi 1979: nos 216, 233 Kukuljevic Diarii, IV/50). Then, in December 1502, the Ottoman *sanjak* of Vlora attempted to capture Butrint (Zamputi 1979: no.260 Kukuljevic-Arkiv Diarii IV/614).

Although Butrint was consistently under the threat of Ottoman incursions, new construction works were rare as the Venetians sought to minimise expenditure in order to ensure profits from the colony were as large as possible. In October 1503, the Venetians determined to convert Butrint into an island (though committing only a small sum of less than 2,000 ducats to the task) by digging a canal 120 paces long across the isthmus to link Lake Butrint with the Vivari Channel. The cost of this new protection would be offset by reducing the number of guards stationed at Butrint (Zamputi 1979: nos 294 Diarii V/362-3). In the event, this project was never realized, repeating a similar scenario at Durrës where plans to turn that city into an island, by the opening of a canal at Porto Romano in c. 1392, had similarly foundered (Thalloczy, Jiricek and Sufflay 1913-18: vol 2, doc 481). As a result of heavy rainfall in December 1502, part of a wall at Butrint collapsed, but there were no resources available for its reconstruction. At the same time in Parga, meanwhile, work to make good the collapse of one of the castle's towers was promptly assessed by an engineer (Zamputi 1979: no 263 Diarii IV/607). The fact that the ancient city's defences were left without repair indicates that the Venetians only used the Acropolis Castle enclosure and the Triangular Fortress, abandoning the lower city.

Venice continued to exploit the wealth of Butrint and in c. 1481 set customs levies on the fish-traps for a ten-year period (Zamputi 1967: doc 73). Timber was also exported from Butrint and stored at Corfu for distribution to other Venetian possessions (Zamputi 1979: nos 291, 294). Stone, too, seems to have been a valuable export commodity.

The economic dependence Venetian Corfu placed upon its mainland dominions emerges in a document as early as 1440, where it is claimed that the island was impoverished in domestic products and that it could survive on its own resources for only three months of the year (Sathas 1882, vol 3: 470). This perilous situation can be seen in a bread crisis on Corfu during October 1503, when the Ottomans were obstructing the export of grain from the mainland, while four months later, grain stored at Delvina was impounded and contracts with the Corfiotes cancelled (Zamputi 1979: nos 300, 356).

During the 15th century Butrint gradually became depopulated because of malaria. In the first decades of the century Butrint (*Vutrendo*) still contained 83 houses, but as time passed the resident population became increasingly reduced. Towards the end of the century, soldiers posted to Butrint to protect the castle and fisheries protested that human cadavers were proliferating sundry diseases (Zamputi 1979: no 111 Diarii, III/776).

In 1537 the Ottoman Sultan Suleiman the Magnificent led a large army against Corfu. Having seized the uplands around Himara the Turks moved south along the Adriatic coast and took Butrint as a base to mount the invasion of Corfu. Ultimately, the plan to invade Corfu failed and, having burned Butrint, Suleiman's army was forced to withdraw (Zamputi 1960). Prior to the Ottoman invasion, a number of defensive construction works were undertaken on Corfu; at Butrint, on the other hand, no such preparations were carried out as the Venetian overlords thought that, either way, Butrint would be unable to withstand the very large and well armed Ottoman army (Marmora 1672: 310).

The retreat of the Turkish army from Corfu was accompanied by a great deal of wilful damage to the area; crops and trees were burned and many buildings and houses were razed. Around 34 years later, the Ionian coastal cities under Venetian control again came under Ottoman threat, this time from Sultan Selim II. Once again Butrint suffered, and both the remains of the city and the castle were in large part destroyed. By this time only one tower of the Triangular Fortress survived and it was no longer thought worthwhile to send large numbers of soldiers to protect the reduced city. Instead, Parga castle was considered a far more suitable site to withstand Ottoman hostility, but even here specialist engineers were required to re-fortify the city as well as 150 troops to protect the site while the construction was undertaken (Marmora 1672: 353). Under the peace accord signed at the end of the 1570-73 Venetian-Ottoman war, Venice ceded Cyprus, but even though nearby Sopot (Borsh) castle was lost to the Ottomans, Butrint remained under Venetian governance.

The Venetians continued to intensively exploit the natural sources of Butrint through the early years of the 17th century. Butrint's coastal fishing grounds were

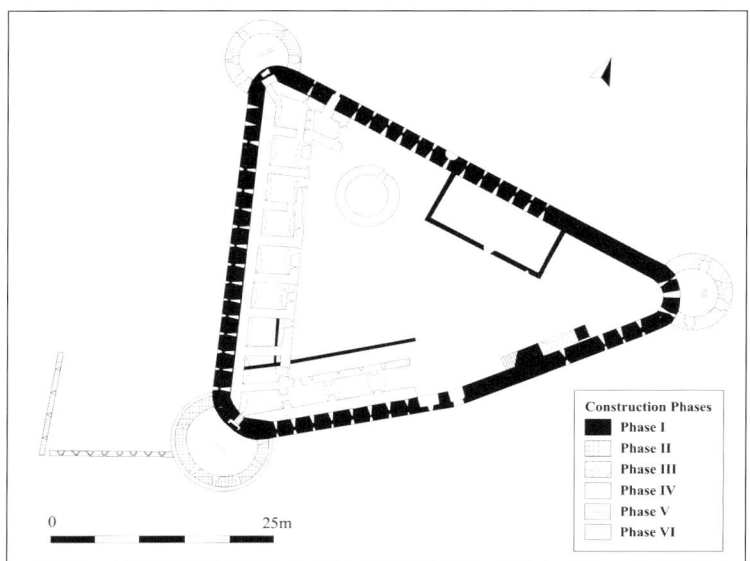

Fig 25 The Triangular Fortress, plan showing construction sequence

granted by licence in five-year periods for up to 60,000 ducats (1616). Local woodlands provided another source of wealth derived from Butrint. In a report from the Venetian governor on Corfu in 1611, it is recorded that a large amount of good quality timber was taken from Butrint, more than enough to prepare cannon firing platforms and other equipment in the Venetian stronghold and to ship the remainder to Crete.

Ottoman interest in the area rarely waned, however, and the 17th century saw the Turks temporarily occupy Butrint on a number of occasions. In 1655 they captured the tower overlooking the fishery, guarded then by 25 men, but the tower was regained by Venetian forces sailing from Corfu in 1660 (Marmora 1672: 423-32). By 1663 the tower was again under the Turks, and sometimes referred to as the 'small castle' (Gratiani 1728, book 32; Nani 1679: 561). By the beginning of the 18th century, Butrint was once more a battleground for Venetian and Ottoman forces. In 1716, Sultan Ahmed III seized Butrint and invaded Corfu. A year later, General Count Mattheus Von Der Schulenburg, commander and acclaimed protector of Corfu during the siege, reclaimed Butrint for Venice with a force of 2,000 men. In the ensuing Peace of Passarowitz, signed on the 27th June 1718, the 'fortress of Butrint' was specified as a possession of the Venetian Republic (Becattini 1788: 249-89).

Butrint remained in Venetian hands until the capitulation of the Republic to Napoleon under the Treaty of Campo Formio on 7th November 1796. After this time, the city fell into the hands of Ali Pasha of Tepelena, who set himself against any possible invasion from the French troops stationed on Corfu. By now the ancient city was entirely abandoned, the fisheries were destroyed and Butrint became a curiosity to visit on a day's sailing from Corfu and a hunting ground for wild game.

The following section concerns the fortifications situated either side of the Vivari Channel, which directly relate to the protection of Butrint when it functioned as a strategic base and fishing centre. The fortifications in question are the Triangular Fortress on the south bank of the channel, the Venetian Tower on the north, city side and the isolated Watchtower overlooking the channel and land approach to the west.

THE TRIANGULAR FORTRESS

The Triangular Fortress on the south bank of the Vivari Channel is reasonably well preserved (Fig. 25, Plates 4 and 72). It has a basic triangular plan with a curve in the centre of its south side. At each of the three corners is a circular tower. Of these, the one at the southwest corner (tower I) is almost wholly intact (Plate 74) while of the remaining two, tower II at the northwest corner is the somewhat better preserved. The fortress has two entrances. The principal gate is in the centre of the south wall, whilst a secondary entrance was opened at a later date in the north wall close to tower II. The walls are generally preserved to (approximately) their original height, around 5 m. The upper level consists of a parapet wall 1.50 m high pierced by numerous firing loops. The parapet walkway is accessed from a staircase built against the south wall close to the main entrance.

Inside the fortress a number of vaulted rooms are built against the west wall and continue on the west side of the south entrance. The rooms were single-storied except for one close to the main gate that had a first floor, forming a kind of internal tower; this does not survive today, but is documented in one of Ugolini's photographs in *Albania Antica* I (Ugolini 1927: 155, fig 107). From this image it can be seen that access to the first floor was controlled through a gate from inside the fortress and that it was lit by a window in the west wall. Within the fortress enclosure there is a freestanding, circular gunpowder warehouse with a tiled roof dating from the latest phase of construction. Outside the fortress, to the west, are the remains of a rectangular enclosure built out from the side of tower I. Today, only the southern extension and parts of the western arm survive. Whilst there is no present indication that the enclosure returned against tower II, this arrangement can be discerned from Ugolini's photographs and the original height of the outer enclosure wall can be estimated.

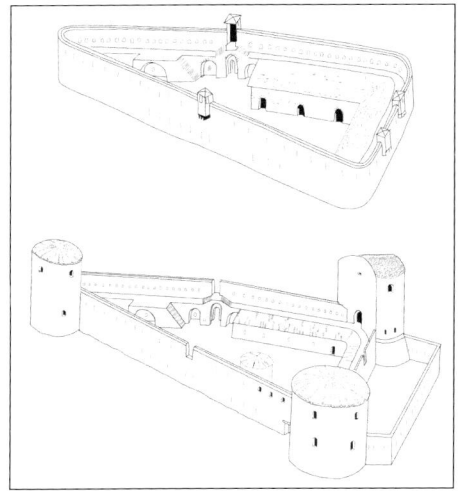

Fig 26 The Triangular Fortress, reconstruction drawings of the fortress in the 14th and 18th centuries

Fig 27 The Triangular Fortress, cannon ports. 1-3: 15th century; 17th century; 18th century

Five main construction phases can be discerned in the Triangular Fortress through examining different construction techniques, the functional needs and aspects of the fort through time, as well as written sources. Only the fortress's three walls can be attributed to the first construction phase; the towers, the internal structures and the gunpowder warehouse are all later additions. Thus, in its original form, the fortress described a plain triangle with rounded corners (Fig. 26).

The evidence for this is that the three corner towers are not tied into the fortress walls, the construction style of the walls and towers is different and in two of the corners firing loops can be seen that were closed off by the construction of the towers. Two blocked loops at parapet level can be seen at the corner with tower I (Plate 73), while at the corner with tower III are two further redundant slits of the ground level band of firing loops (Plate 75). No loops are visible at the corner with tower II as the inner face of the wall is masked by later constructions. In conjunction with construction of the towers, the fortress wall was broken through at each corner to provide internal access. Tower II is architecturally and stylistically similar to tower III and the two belong to the same construction phase. This was preceded by a phase with just a single tower, tower I. The relationship between the first construction phase and the internal structures is rather straightforward, as the internal buildings built over and closed off firing loops at ground level. The development of cannon port design can also be discerned through stylistic comparison (Fig. 27).

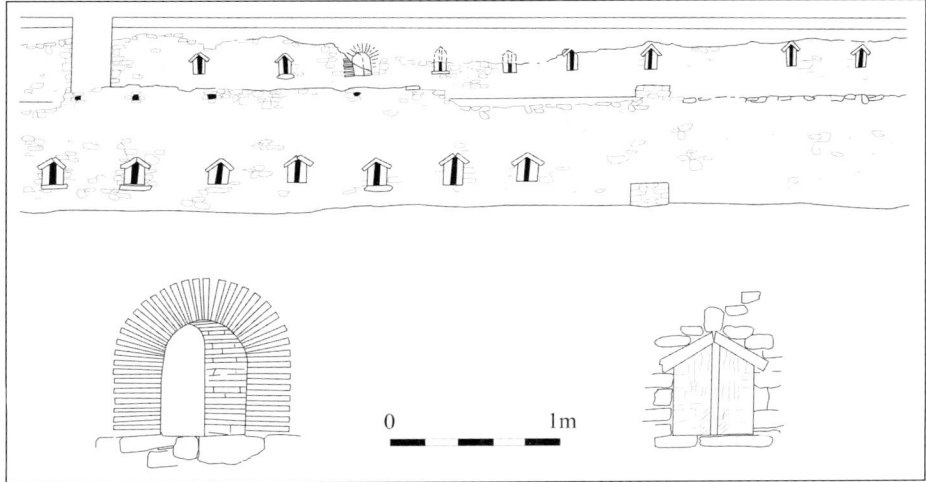

Fig 28 The Triangular Fortress, southwest-facing elevation of the north wall and examples of firing loops

The first construction phase

The walls have a perimeter length of 141.50 m. The shortest side of the triangle (40 m) faces west, while the two other sides are almost equal in length: the north side measures 50 m and the south is 51.50 m. The lower section of the walls is 2.40 m thick and the height to the level of the wall-walk is between 3-3.50 m. The parapet wall is only 0.60 m thick and survives to a height of between 1.50-1.70 m, providing a wall-walk 1.80 m wide. The walls are worked out with small rough-faced stones, measuring typically 0.15 x 0.15 m, and bonded with lime mortar containing coarse inclusions. There are no putlog holes to assess the use of timber scaffolding.

The walls are served by two lines of firing loops. The lower, ground level line pierces the entire thickness of the wall (2.40 m), while the upper line is opened through only the parapet wall (Plate 76). The lower band of loops is set 0.50 m above ground level and between 1-1.40 m apart (Fig. 28). Each wall is provided with 14 to 17 loops. The loops of the lower band are all of the same type, measuring 0.75 m high, 0.50 m wide on the inside and between 0.10-0.20 m wide on the outside (Plate 77). Immediately before reaching the outer wall face they narrow by 40 mm. This characteristic V-shaped construction greatly enlarges the field of fire. Each loop is capped with stone slabs.

The parapet wall firing loops are positioned 0.50 m above the wall-walk; two stylistically different types of loop are present. The first is similar to the ground level loops, capped with stone slabs and measuring 0.50 m high, 0.33 m wide at the inside and 40 mm at the outside. The second type is crowned with brick arches and relates to a separate phase of construction. The first type is the earlier, as the blocked loops at tower I are topped with stone slabs.

In addition to the firing loops, evidence of another early defensive feature can be seen in openings in the parapet in the middle of the north wall (0.94 m wide), in the south wall (0.80 m wide, now blocked), as well as two others in the west wall. These openings were furnished with wooden balconies to act as look-out points over the walls, as the castle was not equipped with towers in its earliest form.

The entrances and staircases

The principal entrance into the fortress in its original form was set in the centre of the south wall at the point where the wall takes a slight bend (Plate 79). Another entrance, 1.08 m wide and later blocked, is situated in the north wall.

The principal entrance is 1.22 m wide and 2.50 m high on the inside of the fort. The actual gateway on the exterior face is lower and constricted to only 0.65 m wide. Both sides of the entrance are topped with arches, rounded on the interior and pointed on the exterior. The exterior gateway is framed with dressed stone blocks. Above the entrance a balcony 0.65 m long was carried on an ornate pair of stone consoles. Only the west side survives, consisting of two shaped stones set one on top of the other. Within the gateway, holes measuring 0.22 x 0.20 m are set 1.65 m above the ground on each side for the attachment and movement of a gate. Inside the fortress, arched recesses are positioned either side of the entrance, one measures 2.40 m wide and the other 2.20 m; both are 1.50 m high. Each is covered by a rounded arch and they penetrate the wall to the same depth as the parapet wall-walk above. Firing loops, to cover the approach to the gate, are set in the middle of each recess. From outside the fortress the technique used to construct the recesses can readily be seen; they were built as arches through the full width of the wall, with the outer face subsequently filled and firing loops let in.

A staircase leading up to the wall-walk is situated on the inside of the south wall to the east of the main entrance. The stairs are carried on an arched structure that is pierced by two firing loops (Fig. 29). The stone steps are 1.50 m wide, with the footers measuring 0.10 x 0.23 m. The staircase is not keyed in to the fortress wall and it is possible that it dates from a later construction period. The location of the loops in the arch also supports this theory, as one appears to be in a particularly unsuitable, cramped position. A second stairway, which more certainly belongs to the first building phase, leads from the wall-walk over the main

The late 13th–19th centuries: Venetian and Ottoman structures

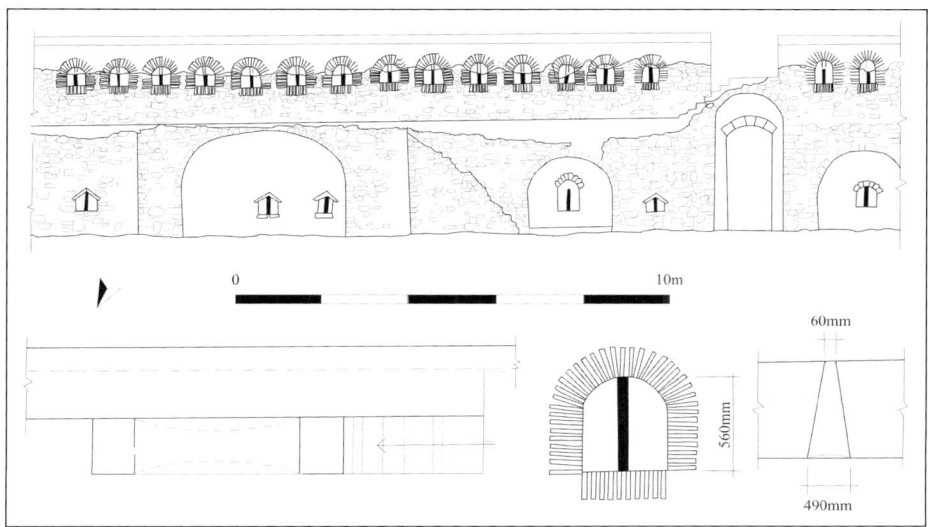

Fig 29 The Triangular Fortress: northwest-facing elevation of the south wall, plan of stairs and example of firing loops

entrance gate to the site of the timber balcony. Only four steps now survive. It is considered that these stair blocks would have been insufficient to serve the entire fortress and that it is likely that timber stairs were also once used.

The internal structures

During light cleaning work inside the fortress, the remains of other walls were found preserved to no more than 0.40 m high. A rectangular structure was discovered built against the face of the north wall (Plate 78). This measures 11.80 x 5.40 m and the walls are 0.50 m thick, consisting of mortared stone with brick fragments. It was covered by a timber roof with a drainage system. To the rear of the structure a section of wall 0.50 m high was added to the inside of the wall-walk in which to set the building's roof timbers; rectangular holes, each 0.20 x 0.20 m square, are spaced 1.10 m apart. The ground level firing loops remained open and presumably therefore in use. The building was entered by a door in the centre of its south wall.

A second wall, with comparable thickness and of similar construction, runs parallel with the south wall of the fortress on the west side and pre-dates the blocks of rooms in the south-west corner. It is aligned 5 m away from the original fortress wall (1.16 m away from the currently standing structures) and continues beneath the rooms on the west side until it meets the fortress's west wall. Within the rooms, another section of wall can be seen running parallel with the western fortress wall. These walls are clearly precursors of the room blocks that can be seen today. The walls may be associated with the remains of a gravel and limestone floor present in parts of the south and west ranges.

The second and third construction phases

Phases 2 and 3 include the addition of the three corner towers and nominally represent a distinction between the substantial tower I and the other two. Tower I, the largest and best preserved of the three, is assigned to the second phase of construction; the modern roof is an acceptable reproduction. The tower is circular in plan with a concave segment on the inside to conform to the corner of the fortress (Fig. 30). The rear wall of the tower is built into the parapet wall but below this the tower walls are not keyed in to the fortress walls. Two firing loops at wall-walk level now face into the tower.

The tower has two stories, both of which were accessed from the rampart wall-walk (Fig. 31). The lower floor sits on a basement 3.10 m high, with its outer walls battered to 15 degrees. The lower room is c. 3 m high and is paved with yellow Venetian tiles. Six cannon ports penetrate the tower wall, which is 1.15 m thick. The ports are covered by tiled arches and taper from 1.06 m wide inside to 0.38 m outside. Their height reduces from 1.16 m inside to 0.64 m outside (cf. Fig. 27.3).

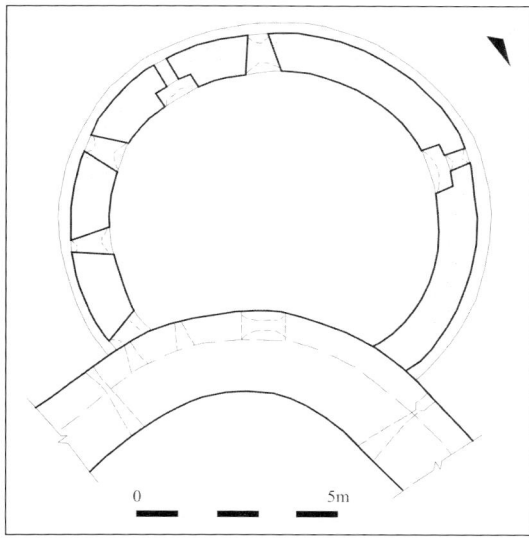

Fig 30 The Triangular Fortress, plan of the lower storey of tower 1

The upper storey, probably a residential space, was supported on a timber floor carried on a 0.20 m wide projection. The two storeys were linked by an internal wooden staircase. The upper floor was lit by three large windows decorated with tiled arches and frames (Plate 80). One window opens on to the inside of the fortress whilst the remaining two look west and east respectively. There are also six narrow tile-lined firing loops. A broad chimney on the south wall tapers from 1.20 m wide at its base to 0.38

m at the top. Like the windows and loops, the sides of the chimney are framed with tiles. The north and south sections of the tower wall are raised to create an apex to hang a timber and tile roof; this was supported on an apron of three to four brick courses.

Externally, the tower walls consist of roughly dressed stone set in courses and carefully bonded with strong mortar. The lower, battered section of the tower is divided from the vertical upper section by a decorative line of faced stones, 0.26 m high and projecting 60 mm from the wall face. The windows and loops are also fitted out decoratively with stone or tile surrounds. Equipped with artillery pieces, the tower commanded the approaches to Butrint looking towards the sea, the land route from Ksamil and across the Vrina Plain to the south.

Though perhaps not separated by a great period of time, tower I differs entirely from towers II and III in its architecture and construction technique. It is impossible to be certain whether tower I pre- or post-dates the other two, but towers II and III are more certainly contemporaneous. They bear the same shape, plan and construction technique. Both towers are circular with vertical walls and are built from larger materials than other parts of the fortification. The stones are almost square and are laid in courses. Both towers abut the first phase fortress walls. Entrances are knocked through the fortress's corners at ground level to access the towers. Traces of a number of firing loops were found whilst cleaning the crumbling masonry.

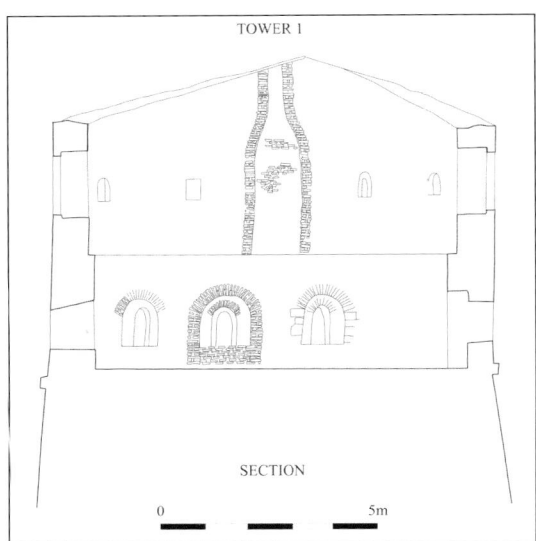

Fig 31 The Triangular Fortress, section through tower 1

Tower II is preserved up to 4 m high, corresponding approximately to the floor level of its upper storey (Plate 81). The walls of the ground floor are 1.70 m thick and strengthened by timber braces (Fig. 32). The internal diameter of the tower is 5.40 m (Fig. 33). The ground floor entrance to the tower from the fortress measures 1.50 x 1.15 m. The floor itself sat above a foundation 0.80 m high and was carried on a stone projection set 0.20 m out from the wall. Four stone-arched

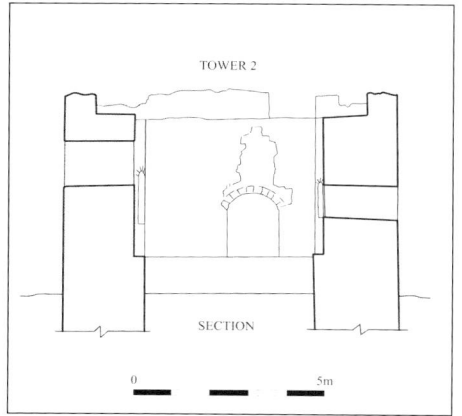
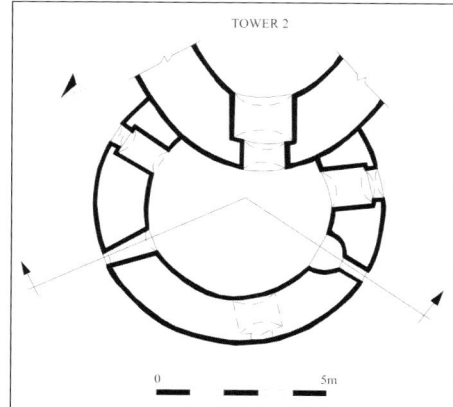

Fig 32 The Triangular Fortress, section through tower 2

Fig 33 The Triangular Fortress, plan of the ground floor of tower 2

cannon ports are set in the wall and, at its highest point, a sloping window allowed the maximum amount of light to penetrate to the floor. The cannon ports are rectangular or semicircular in plan, narrowing 1.20 m to 0.30-0.60 m from inside to out. Similarly, they reduce in height from 1.20 m to 1-1.10 m. One port is blocked with bonded stone masonry and another with dry bricks. The dimensions, fabric and colour (light ochre) of the bricks are similar to those used in the firing loops of the western outwork.

The wall of the upper storey is 0.65 m thick, though it is not well preserved. On the north side traces of a semicircular chimney remain. The upper storey was probably a living space and had its own entrance on to the parapet walk. The inside of the room was plastered and its floor was paved with ochre-coloured bricks set in a bed of mortar. No other architectural elements (firing loops, windows, etc) can be discerned at this level, but from the narrowness of the wall it seems unlikely that there would have been another storey above it. The tower was originally capped with a tiled roof, as suggested by the many tiles found during excavations (with identical dimensions and forms as modern examples), alongside Islamic pottery fragments, clay tobacco pipes and cannonballs with a diameter of 50-60 mm.

Tower III survives to only 2 m high (Plate 83). It was found filled by demolition debris from the upper levels. After cleaning, three round arched cannon ports emerged, each rectangular in plan but otherwise with similar tapering dimensions to those in tower II. The wooden floor of the lower storey was supported on a foundation projecting 0.25 m inside the tower and rising 0.90 m from ground level.

Remains of a semicircular chimney were also found in the ground floor wall. During cleaning works large quantities of tiles, ceramic tobacco pipes and two Venetian coins of the late 17th century were found.

The fourth construction phase

The fourth construction phase concerns the fortress's internal structures built against the south and west walls as well as some elements of the parapet level firing loops. The construction style of the two ranges of buildings differs entirely from anything anywhere else in the fortress, and markedly so from that in towers II and III. The walls are built of small stones, set irregularly and bonded with mortar. Dressed stones are only used in roof vaulting and door frames.

The south range is built against the interior face of the fortress, is 2.60 m wide and composed of parallel walls 0.75m thick. The range is sub-divided into four rooms and supports a single vaulted roof. The room closest to the fortress's main entrance does not survive intact, but photographs from Ugolini's archive indicate that it carried another storey above. The next room to the west measures 2.60 x 4.40 m and communicates with the first via a doorway; two firing loops face into the fortress. The third room is connected to the second by a door and has a separate door and accompanying loop into the fortress interior. The fourth and final room is accessed only from the third and has no other lighting. As with the south range, the rooms of the west range are built against the interior fortress wall, closing off the original ground level firing loops and partly obscuring those at the parapet. The west range consists of three larger spaces, 4 m wide, covered by individual vaulted ceilings. Two of the rooms have a conjoining internal door and six doors with adjacent loops open from the range on to the inside of the fortress.

The gate in the north wall of the Triangular Fortress close to tower II, together with a complex of defended chambers behind it, belongs to the fourth phase of construction. The gate opens into a rectangular space fitted with four firing loops, one of which looks into the interior of the fortress. A second gate allows access to the ground floor of tower II. The complex is entered from inside the fortress via an arched entrance (Plate 82) adorned with a small carved relief of the head of the Lion of St Mark (Plate 84).

A freestanding circular gunpowder magazine (Plate 85), with a diameter of 4.50 m and walls 1.15 m thick, was built in the northwest part of the fortress. The magazine has a door on the north side and a domed roof originally clad with tiles or stone slabs.

Certain firing loops on the parapet, though of unequal dimensions, are framed by tile surrounds and belong to the fourth phase of construction. The cannon ports in this style represent a great improvement on the earlier phases. Restored first phase loops can be seen in the north wall close to tower II and examples can also be seen in the somewhat reduced parapet of the west wall. The phenomenon can best be observed in the south wall where the repair or replacement of earlier loops, with tile framed loops and ports, is most common. Towards the base of the west wall, close to tower II, a broad port topped with an arch of characteristically similar bricks was let in, measuring 0.84 m wide at the outside and 0.80 m high.

The loops, designed for hand-held weapons, are usually of simple triangular section, 0.50 m wide on the inside narrowing to 0.16 m on the outside and are generally c. 0.55 m high. The cannon ports include two variant forms. The first, measuring 0.40 m wide on the inside, splays to 0.60 m on the outside. An example in the north wall close to tower II cuts obliquely through the parapet, facing northwest towards the seaward approach, a direction of possible threat. The second form, seen adjacent to the example above, comprises an hourglass shape, first tapering and then broadening out once more (cf. Fig. 27.1). The north wall example measures 0.73 m wide at the outside, 0.43 m in the middle and 0.64 m at the inside. Two further ports of the same type in the eastern half of the south fort wall were later blocked in.

The fifth construction phase: extramural additions to the fortress
The final phase of construction at the Triangular Fortress concerns an extramural addition to the fortress: the western outwork (cf. Fig. 30). Originally approximately rectangular in shape, its remains abut the outer face of tower I; a parallel section of the wall, now lost but documented by Ugolini, abutted tower II. The resultant enclosure measured 43 x 14 m. The intention of the new enclosure, it seems, was to provide a forward firing line for riflemen.

Conversely, having now lost its purpose, a cannon port in tower II facing into the enclosure was blocked with light ochre-coloured bricks left over from construction of the western outwork loops. The tower window was blocked around the same time, indicating that the interior of the structure was no longer used as it had once been. Moreover, a rough-built stone staircase constructed on the fortress interior, close to the tower, masked one of the firing loops designed to guard the complex behind the small northern gate/tower entrance.

Today, only a short L-shaped section of the outwork survives attached to tower I. This measures 14 m east to west and 11.50 m north to south. On average the wall is preserved to a height of 2.20 m, only in one place reaching 3.20m. The wall is 0.53 m thick, and comprised of roughly faced limestone blocks bound with small stones or brick pieces inserted into the mortar. The outwork is pierced by firing loops 0.60 m high and set 1.22 m above ground level. The loops are fashioned from ochre-coloured bricks and are capped by stone slabs. These are similar to the loops of the Venetian Tower on the opposite side of the channel in their construction style, shape, dimension and brick colour. There are nine double firing loops in the south wall of the outwork, while in the west wall only four single loops survive.

The Venetian Tower and the Watchtower

Two isolated towers still stand on the north bank of the Vivari Channel. One of them, the impressive Venetian Tower, is situated opposite the Triangular Fortress, whilst the Watchtower is perched on rocks some 300 m to the west.

The Venetian Tower

The Venetian Tower is very well preserved (Fig. 34, Plate 4). Of the original structure only its roof, door and drawbridge, as well as the wooden ladder between floors are missing. The square tower is built over two floors on top of a lower battered section 4.30 m high (Fig. 35). The walls are faced with rough-dressed stonework with more fine stones used at the corners. The junction between the battered section and that above is marked by four courses of red bricks standing 60 mm proud from the wall and with dressed masonry blocks at each corner. The interior of the basement is filled with soil and stone rubble. In order to reduce the outward pressure of the fill and to provide greater resistance to artillery fire, the basement is sub-divided by four cross walls, each 0.50 m thick. Mortar is carefully applied to produce a surface as smooth as possible.

The top of the tower is finished with a well-crafted decorative device consisting of seven brick courses, each successive course projecting out from that below. The same bricks are also used on the edges of the firing loops and in a window arch. In the southern façade there is a window on each floor as well as two firing loops placed one either side of the lower floor window. The door to the tower is in the eastern face and is accessed via a twisting stone staircase and timber drawbridge (Plate 86). A firing loop is set on each side of the door. The upper floor on the east side is served by four loops. A fifth, centrally placed slit, is set below the line of the others; this is not a firing loop, but carried the drawbridge chains, via a channel in the upper storey floor, down to the winding mechanism on the lower floor. The north and west faces both have a band of four loops each per floor except for the upper storey on the north side which has five.

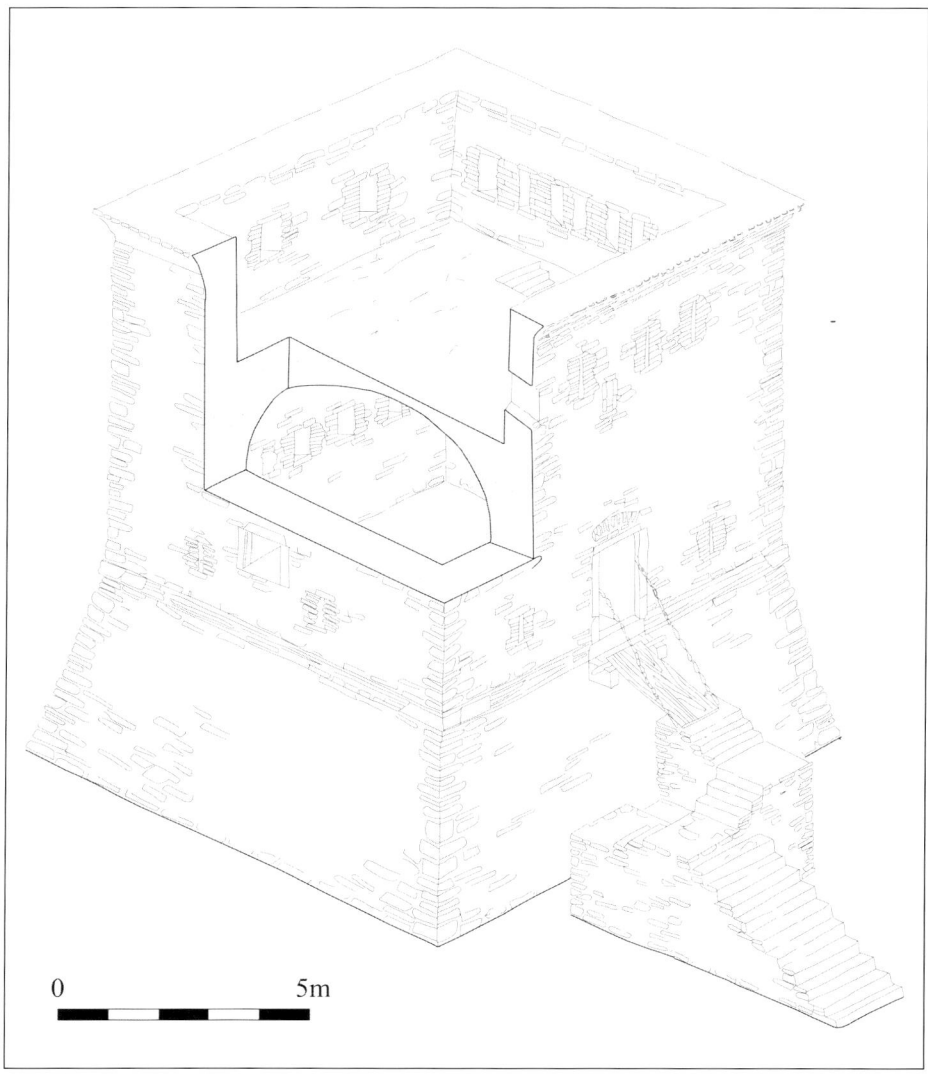

Fig 34 The Venetian Tower, isometric reconstruction

The lower floor of the tower consists of a 6 x 6 m square structure with 1 m thick walls. It is covered by a crossed brick vault 0.30 m thick. Floor to vault top/ceiling height is 2.50 m. A foundation offset, 0.50 m high in the wall, indicates where the beams of the original floor were suspended. Close to the north wall a space in the ceiling measuring 1 x 1.80 m allowed for a wooden spiral staircase to the upper floor.

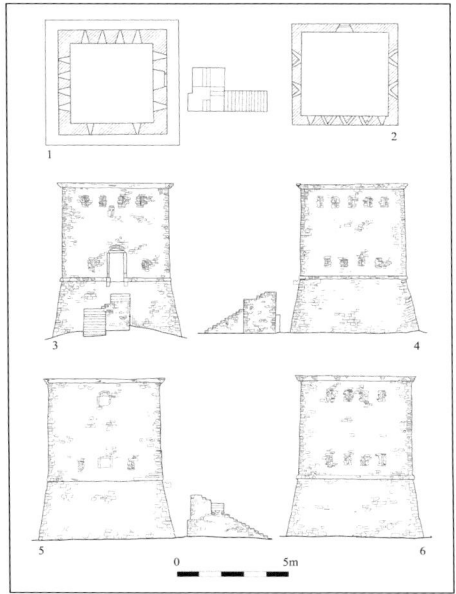
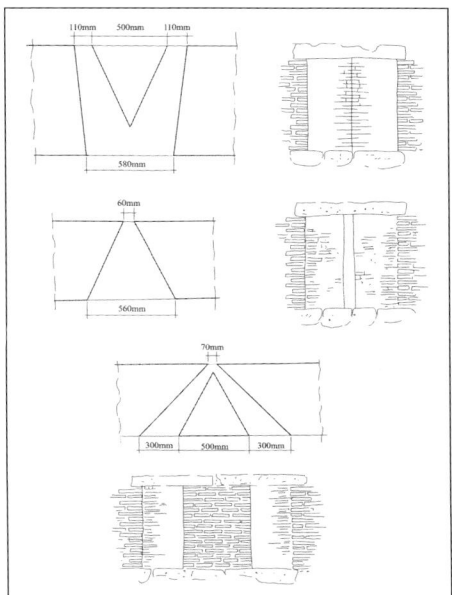

Fig 35 The Venetian Tower: 1. plan of lower storey; 2. plan of upper storey; 3. east-facing elevation; 4. north-facing elevation; 5. south-facing elevation; 6. west-facing elevation

Fig 36 The Venetian Tower, plans and elevations of firing loops

The lower storey firing loops are all of the same form, set 1.12 m above the floor, 0.56 m high and tapering from 0.53 m wide inside to 0.10 m outside. The firing loops are capped by flat stone slabs and edged with bricks. The window in the south wall is 0.77 m wide and 0.88 m high. On the exterior the window is framed by dressed stone blocks that carry hinge fittings from the original shutters. Inside, the window is crowned with a brick arch and is edged in brick. The sill slopes downwards to permit more light to reach the floor.

The lower storey doorway is 1.10 m wide x 1.90 m high. It is framed externally with carefully dressed stonework and finished with a stone lintel. On the interior, the entrance is covered by a simple brick arch. The upper edges of the entrance are also finished with bricks.

The external stone stair block is situated 1.60 m apart from the doorway and the two were linked via a drawbridge. The drawbridge was supported on the upper platform of the stairs and articulated on two limestone corbels set beneath the tower door. As noted above, the drawbridge chains were manoeuvred through a slit high above the doorway. The raised drawbridge covered a set of double doors secured by a bolt.

The upper floor of the tower comprises a square space 6.25 x 6.25 m with walls 0.75 m thick. The upper floor is suspended on the arch built over the storey below and is preserved to its original height of 2.45 m. On the upper part of the walls the remnants of wooden beams that originally supported the roof structure survive. Matching the floor below, the upper storey was lit by a single centrally placed window in the south face; elsewhere the walls are equipped with firing loops.

There are matching pairs of firing loops in the east and west walls, each loop divided by triangular wedges of bricks to produce two apertures to the outside (Fig. 36). This type of double loop commands a wide field of fire. A typical loop measures 0.65 x 0.58 m on the inside, splitting into two 0.10 m wide openings on the outside. The loops are built of brick and capped with stone slabs. The slit in the east wall to take the drawbridge chains is 0.11 m wide and 0.60 m high and is edged in dressed stone blocks. The five apertures of the loops opening on the north side of the upper floor are of mixed design. The outer two are of the simple type used on the lower floor. The remaining three are double loops split by wedges but are the opposite of the loops in the west wall in that they each have two firing positions and only one exit point. This manner of construction enabled a crossfire over the area leading from the ancient city.

It is notable that the form, dimensions, construction style and the ochre-coloured bricks in the Venetian Tower firing loops are similar to the later additions in the Triangular Fortress parapet wall. It is also worth noting that the greatest number of firing loops is in the north side of the tower, facing the city of Butrint.

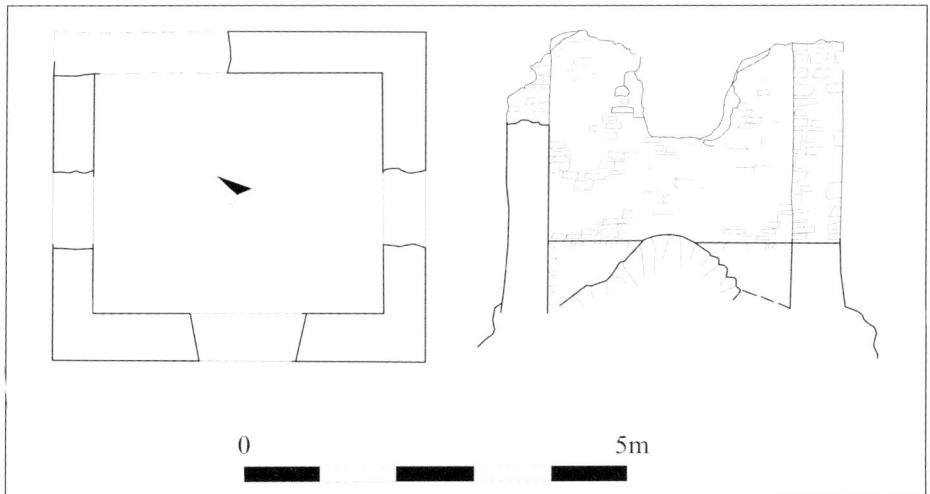

Fig 37 The Watchtower, plan and southeast-facing elevation

The southern face, on the other hand, was protected by the Triangular Fortress and was lit by large windows instead. This evidence demonstrates that the tower was intended to protect the channel's north bank from the highest points of Butrint as well as from the seaward approach. At the time the tower was built the fortified walls of Butrint survived to little more than ground level in this area; the tower itself, and its stair block, were constructed over the line of the earlier defences.

The Watchtower

The Watchtower is situated on a prominent rock outcrop above the steep north bank of the Vivari Channel some 300 m west of the Venetian Tower (Plates 3 and 87). From this point it surveys the whole of the channel from Butrint to its outfall at the sea and the landward approach to Butrint from the direction of the modern road (Plate 88).

The tower is rectangular, 2.90 x 2.44 m, with walls 0.44-0.50 m thick (Fig. 37). The walls rise up out of the landscape, built of small rough stones bonded with lime mortar with fine inclusions. The walls were originally rendered, both inside and out, and survive up to 2 m high. The single chamber within the tower took the natural bedrock as its floor and was entered by a door in the north side of which little now remains.

In the centre of the south wall the traces of a 1 m wide wooden balcony can be discerned in a timber setting in the masonry beneath the balcony entrance. Both side walls were originally served by a window, though these too are now all but lost. The windows, together with the viewing platform of the balcony, afforded a broad lookout on many of the approaches to the Triangular Fort and the Venetian Tower that controlled navigation between the sea and Lake Butrint.

DATING THE CHANNEL-SIDE FORTIFICATIONS

The style of the earliest construction phase of the Triangular Fortress is different from Butrint's Byzantine fortification systems and from the 'true' Venetian constructions, falling somewhere between the two. For example, timber lookout balconies were common in the West during the 12th to 13th centuries (Meyer 1968). In Albania, these structures were used at the 15th-century castle of Bashtova, the lower castle in Durrës as well as at Petrela. We know that the Angevin Charles I (self-proclaimed king of Albania 1272-85) equipped the walls of Durrës with such features in *c*. 1280, while parapets incorporating firing loops appeared by the end of the 13th century and were used widely during the 14th century (Thalloczy, Jiricek and Sufflay 1913-18: vol 1, 27 May 1280; Toy 1955). Moreover, the thickness and greater height of the walls of the Triangular Fortress in comparison to Butrint's medieval walls, suggest that the fort was constructed for the age of gunpowder artillery, perhaps in the early era of its use, around the last quarter of the 14th century to the early 15th century. A Venetian map depicting the area around Vlora Bay shows that the old fortress on the acropolis had been destroyed by the Turks in 1571 and a new and smaller fortification built by 1655 (AA.VV. 1998: 47, fig 174a). The latter is identifiable with the Triangular Fotress, though if the Turks merely reinforced an existing tower or built a completely new fort is unclear.

The Watchtower may belong to the same period of fortification building at Butrint. Similar to the campanile at the entrance of the monastery in Mesopotam, its thin walls resemble an Angevin construction more than a Venetian building. Both the Watchtower and Triangular Fortress are built of stone rather than brick and both use wooden balconies, possibly as machicolations (hoardings). The Watchtower primarily served as a warning and signalling station to the fort's garrison

Tower I of the Triangular Fortress is, architecturally, a true Venetian construction. Characteristics of these buildings include: battered foundations filled with soil to the level of the first floor; dressed stone corners; and stone bands to divide architectural elements and decorate façades. In its dimensions and firing loops, it is similar to Venetian towers of the 15th century. However, some elements such as the rectangular form of the decorative stone band and the use of yellow bricks in the windows and floors lead to the conclusion that it was built around the 17th century.

The remaining two towers in the fortress have nothing in common with typical Venetian constructions. Their vertical walls, the low height they rise above the curtain walls, the use of wooden braces in residential areas and the style of the cannon ports all imply that the towers relate to the Ottoman period, more inspired by Byzantine fortresses than Western European examples. For instance, the same type of cannon port is also found at Ishmi castle (northwest of Kruja), an Ottoman period fortification constructed in *c*. 1573. Meanwhile, typical examples of earlier Ottoman cannon ports are completely different, such as those in Elbasan castle that date from the reconstruction of 1466, and are characteristic 15th-century forms.

The south and west ranges in the Triangular Fortress and the guarded entrance complex to tower II are more reminiscent of 18th-19th century fortifications in Albania, such as the castles of Porto Palermo, Paleokastra, Tepelena, etc. Indeed, these late constructions could readily be attributed to Ali Pasha of Tepelena, one of the last governors of Butrint, were it not for the Lion of St Mark relief above the tower II complex entrance. The latest construction at the fortress is the western outwork. Based on comparison of dimensions and the use of bricks in the firing loops, this wall appears to be contemporary with the Venetian Tower on the opposite bank of the channel. The common architectural features of the Venetian

Tower and outwork, namely the double firing loops, push their construction date towards the 18th-19th centuries.

Overall, through considering the construction periods of the fortifications alongside the Vivari Channel, the conclusion must be that the importance of Butrint gradually diminished as the area became less readily controlled. This was first suggested by the construction of the Triangular Fortress towers II and III and later the siting of gun ports facing the city. In the building of the Venetian Tower, too, the imperative of pointing guns towards the city is clear to see.

Having established the phased and dated architectural descriptions of the channel-side fortifications, we can now attempt to situate these within historical events.

It is clear thus far that the first phase of the Triangular Fortress bears no comparison to the architectural features of Butrint's Byzantine fortifications, a campaign of building that ceased with the demise of the Despotate of Epirus. The inclusion of Butrint within the Despotate denied Western influence in the city's architecture, a phenomenon that did not occur at some sites in central Greece. Influence from the West is only evident in Butrint's architecture from the time of Angevin possession (the end of the 13th century), and especially during the time of Venetian dominion (the end of the 14th to the end of the 18th century). These later constructions were limited in number and extent, however, as the importance of the city waned; this also explains why, unlike at Durrës, local influence can not be seen in the military architecture at Butrint. The Triangular Fortress was undoubtedly influenced by Western designs and Butrint was one of the most important bases for the Angevins on the Albanian coast, serving as a starting point for incursions into the interior.

At the end of the 13th century the fortified walls of Butrint would have been slighted and no longer defensively effective. It is suggested that initially the Angevin forces might have occupied the Acropolis Castle constructed by Michael II whilst the Triangular Fortress and Watchtower were constructed. This makes sense of the definition of Butrint in Angevin texts as a '*Castrum*' (Ducellier 1981: 43). Angevin domination was particularly strong in coastal southern Albania and a succession of Angevin commanders is recorded at Butrint, such as Hyget, Lougevilet, etc (Ducellier 1981: 261). Angevin influence is marked at the nearby monastery church of Shën Koll at Mesopotam, especially in the decorative sculpture such as the depiction of lilies on floor slabs (Meksi 1972; 1975b).

The Triangular Fortress is a hastily made fortress that did not meet established military standards of the day. The relatively low walls and the absence of towers are not characteristic of the end of the 13th or early 14th centuries. The earliest documentation of the fortress is in 1572 when it is described as a tower protecting the lake fisheries (Marmora 1672: 353). Given the 'tower' description, it is likely that tower I had been erected by this time. In his encyclopaedia of 1688, Camocio also describes a tower on the south bank of the Vivari where the Triangular Fortress is located. Based on assessment of its architectural features alone, tower I would have been constructed around the end of the 15th century. The reason for building such structures at this time was because the Venetian overlords feared the threat posed to both Corfu and Butrint by the Ottoman navy.

Historical sources inform us that on 20th May 1655 the castle of Vivari was overrun by Turks, who thereby gained control over Butrint's rich fishing grounds (Marmora 1672: 422). The Ottomans besieged Butrint with a great number of foot soldiers and cavalry, bringing in cannon from Delvina. The occupying Venetian force and fishermen abandoned the fort leaving only the commander with five men and his family. Though a letter was sent to Corfu requesting reinforcements of men and munitions, nothing arrived. The defensive walls were damaged and ineffective, and the Ottomans captured the city (Marmora 1672: 423). In 1656 the fort contained a small garrison of 50 men and two artillery pieces. Guards were set in the 'tower' and the 'old fortress'. The Ottomans apparently established Butrint as a royal castle (*Poi fabbricarono ivi presso una fortezza reale*), and though they did not carry out alleged plans to build a new fort, the Triangular Fortress was repaired (Marmora 1672: 431). It is possible that the Ottomans did not actually build towers II and III, and that references to building works around this time refer to reconstitution of the old walls of the Triangular Fortress, returning it to a defensible condition.

In 1660, Butrint was once more at the centre of conflict between the Ottomans and Venetians. Venetian Corfu hoped to regain Butrint and with it the fisheries. Spies were sent to report on the condition of the Triangular Fortress and how it might be retaken. Deciding against direct conflict, a plan of diplomacy and deceit was adopted. According to Andrea Marmora, the historian of Corfu, having sailed three boats up the channel the Corfiote captain Barbati lured the Ottoman commander out of the fort on the pretext of offering gifts and negotiations. Venetian troops, concealed in surrounding woods, then launched a surprise attack on the fort. The Venetians brought up artillery to threaten the occupants and lit fires around the fort to smoke them out. The Ottomans surrendered the following day and the Venetians moved in a garrison of 200 men (Marmora 1672: 432-33).

In 1716 Butrint was once more in Ottoman hands, seized as a springboard to mount assaults on the kingdoms of Naples and Sicily (Becattini 1788: 210). Corfu was first in the firing line, offering the potential as a base for their future plans (Becattini 1788: 214). The Venetian and Ottoman fleets engaged in the Straits of Corfu and then, on 20th August 1716 after a month-long siege, the Turks withdrew with great losses (According to Becattini (1788: 223), the Ottomans left 20,000 dead soldiers on the battlefield though this claim seems greatly exaggerated). Retaking the initiative in 1717 and reinforced by the Portuguese navy, the Venetians sent a force of 2,000 soldiers under the command of General Von Der Schulenburg to capture Butrint (Becattini 1788: 249).

Following these events the Venetians undertook fortification works for the provision of their garrison, and after this time the internal structures and small entrance close to tower II were built. Perhaps some little time later, the extramural rectangular enclosure was built between towers I and II, around the same time the Venetian Tower was built on the opposite bank.

The Triangular Fortress, though lacking the accoutrements of contemporary fortifications, remained very important to Venetian Butrint to the end of the 18th century. Subsequent to the Treaty of Campo Formio on 17th October 1797, which ratified Napoleon Bonaparte's subjugation of the Venetian Republic, French troops from a detachment based on Corfu occupied the Triangular Fortress. Much of what we know of the fortress from this time is drawn from the descriptions left by a French infantry captain, J.P. Bellaire (Bellaire 1805: 129-31). The castle was strengthened with three towers and encircled by water channels. Artillery pieces were positioned in the lower storeys of the towers whilst the upper storeys were used to accommodate officers and other men of the garrison. Inside the fortress were a small barracks and a number of warehouses, but it is hard to see how the decrepit fortress could have accommodated the stated garrison of 100 men. The parapets and firing loops were in poor order, unfit for purpose, though a protected firing platform (perhaps a *ravelin*), was built in front of the south entrance.

Bellaire, probably quoting from Marmora, mentions that the fortress of Butrint was originally a tower constructed by Michael II (Despotate of Epirus), which was later reconstructed by the Turks on a grander scale.[8] After the siege of Corfu in 1716, the fortress was refurbished under Schulenburg as a military outpost from which to garner provisions for the Venetian fleet (Bellaire 1805: 131). Bellaire recounts the presence of several towers at Butrint that were used by the Venetian military. One of these towers, the most significant during a confrontation between French troops and the forces of Ali Pasha of Tepelena, was the tower of 'Xhako'. This name probably refers to Jaco [Vrina], and hence to a tower situated on the hill exposed above the marshes now occupied by the modern village of Vrina, some 2 km down the Pavllas River from the Triangular Fortress (Plate 3). The French writer François

---

8   Editor's note: there is often confusion in deciphering the historic references. The "tower" of Michael II is generally taken to mean the Acropolis Castle – and not the Triangular Fortress – although the possibility that a watchtower or blockhouse preceded the Triangular Fortress can not be discounted.

Pouqueville mentions another isolated fortification, the tower of Gonemi, located by the coast close to the outfall of the Vivari Channel (Pouqueville 1820, vol 1: 369).

Some of Bellaire's remarks, however, can not be taken on trust. His description of artillery in the corner towers in conjunction with the western outwork proposes an unlikely scenario; are we to conclude, therefore, that the outwork was not constructed until after 1798 and with it the contemporary Venetian Tower? Bellaire's observation of a 'Greek chapel' in Butrint and parapets on the castle walls are equally questionable.

With the arrival of the French on Corfu in June 1797, the French general Gentile met with Ali Pasha to secure Butrint and the former Venetian mainland possessions. The Pasha's request to station a number of ships in the Ionian Sea was rebuffed, but Gentile did provide a number of artillery officers and permitted Ali some boats off the Butrint peninsula with the objective of mollifying him into cooperation (Boppe 1914: 7; Remerand 1928: 27). However, Napoleon's war with Egypt dragged the Ottomans into conflict with the French in September 1798. Assessing the strength of the opposing Anglo-Russo-Turkish coalition, Ali Pasha made his own plans. Arriving for negotiations near Filati [Filiates, near Igoumenitsa], Ali arrested the French representative from Corfu and set in motion a strategy to seize the coastal fortifications of Butrint, Preveza and Vonitsa (Alcairi 1823: 70). The French commander of Butrint withstood Ali's attempts to deceive him into submission and possession was ultimately decided in a battle between 17th to 26th October 1798 (Remerand 1928: 58).

During the first night, Ali Pasha's Albanian forces sealed off all of the access routes to the Triangular Fortress (Bellaire 1805: 261). French reinforcements were requested and sent from Corfu in the shape of two companies of grenadiers and a detachment of military engineers. From Bellaire's description of events, it seems that the French landed somewhere between the fortress and Pavllas River and, with assistance from the fort's garrison, they managed to take temporary control of the nearby hills. However, around 100 of Ali's soldiers were securely positioned in the Tower of Jaco and could not be expelled. The French commander M. Petit called for a further 300 men equipped with artillery. The fresh reinforcement was lead by General Chabot, and subsequently General Vernier, who took command of the battle from the Triangular Fortress. Meanwhile, the Pasha's forces also continued to grow. The French forward troops were concentrated on the hillsides about 3 km from the fortress and aimed to take the Tower of Jaco. The tower was assaulted with artillery and grenadier charges but without success. Ali's troops counter-attacked from across the Pavllas and put the French to flight.

Despite having the advantages of arms and terrain the French took heavy losses, and with the generals themselves in danger of capture Chabot gave orders for a general withdrawal. On 24th October 1798 the French headquarters on Corfu decided to destroy the fortress at Butrint. The following day, a detachment of artillerymen and soldiers shelled tower III and burned out towers I and II as well as some of the internal buildings. On 26th October 1798 Butrint finally fell under Ali Pasha's control. In the following February the Russo-Turkish navy forced the French out from Corfu (Zamputi 1967: 457). Butrint and its Triangular Fortress remained under Ali Pasha until 18th August 1820, when he was captured by the Turkish army (Isambert 1873: 835). During his occupation of Butrint, Ali Pasha fortified a building by the mouth of the Vivari Channel to create a new castle.

ALI PASHA'S CASTLE

At the mouth of the Vivari Channel where it opens into the Ionian Sea, a castle sits on the north, channel side, of a small island (Plate 3). Ali Pasha of Tepelena selected this site to secure control of the channel and the seaward approach to Butrint. The castle is rectangular in plan, measuring 30 x 22 m, and provided with a tower at each corner (Fig. 38). The towers facing the sea (west) are circular whilst the other two are rectangular. The principal entrance is set between the rectangular towers and a second, narrower entrance is situated centrally in the north wall facing the channel. The towers overlooking the sea are provided with firing embrasures.

The walls

The castle walls are 1.40 m thick and survive up to their original height of 5.10 m on the west and south sides. The north, and particularly the south, walls are less well preserved. The wall foundations are thicker by 0.60 m than the upper parts and have battered external faces. The height of the walls and towers are the same, in common with other fortifications of Ali Pasha. The walls consist of small rough-cut stones bonded with lime mortar. Only the west side, facing threat from the sea, is built more thoughtfully, with dressed rectangular blocks and, in comparison to other of Ali's fortifications, the Vivari castle seems to have been built in haste. The walls are equipped with firing loops at battlements level and there is a viewing porthole in the south wall adjacent to tower I (Fig. 39, Plate 91).

The towers

Of the castle's four towers the two circular structures on the west are the most powerful. The upper sections of the tower walls are 2 m thick; their lower sections, like the curtain walls, are battered outwards. The upper decks are fitted with large

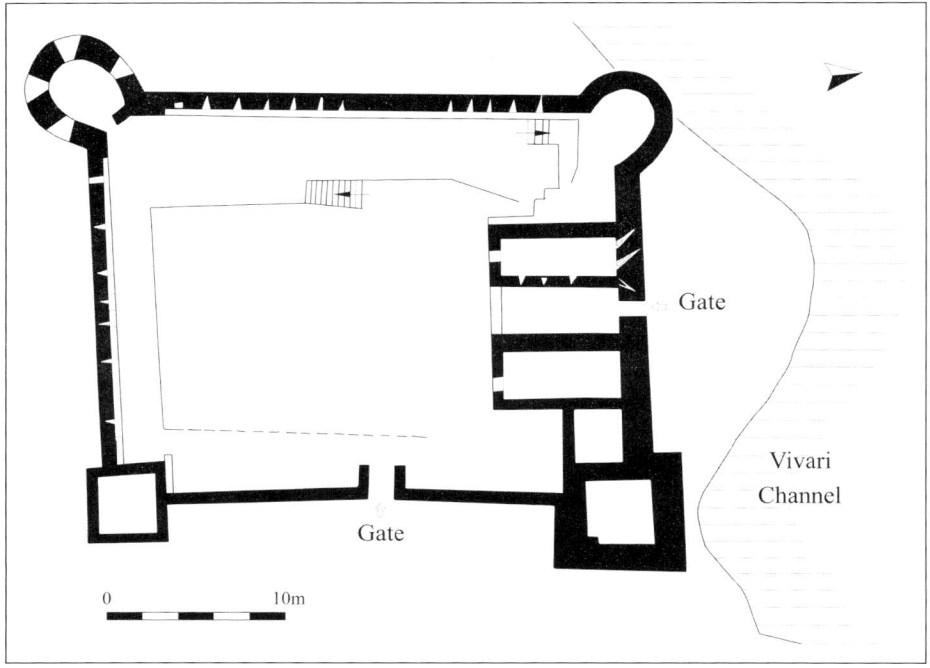

Fig 38 Ali Pasha's Castle

cannon embrasures, in which can be seen iron attachment pegs. The cannon embrasures survive completely in the southwest tower (tower I), (Plate 89), where four openings dominate three sides of the horizon: to the north, west and south. The embrasures splay from 0.80 m inside to between 2.40-3.10 m outside enabling the cannon, which sat within the walls of the tower, to look directly along the castle walls. The firing platform was surfaced with a wooden floor. The 1 m wide entrance to the tower does not communicate directly with the parapet wall-walk, rather it was accessed via a ladder. The ground floor below the gun platform could only have been used as a storehouse. The tower was covered by a conical wooden roof though no traces of this survive. The circular tower in the northwest corner, tower II, is of the same construction, but survives only up to the base of the embrasures.

Tower III, the southeast tower, survives up to the original wall height of 5.10 m (Plate 90). Only the wooden roof is missing. Tower III is the least exposed to possible attack, located furthest from the sea and the Vivari Channel. The lower half of its exterior is battered with a 30° slope. The tower's ground floor has a vaulted roof and is not accessible from the upper floor. The upper level measures 4.50 x 4.60 m and its wall is between 0.40–0.50 m thick. The entrance to the upper floor is in the north wall and is 0.90 m wide. A stone bench (3.0 x 1.10 m), outside the entrance door is accompanied by a stone staircase up to the first floor entrance.

Tower IV is similar in plan to tower III though its dimensions are larger, 8 m on the north side and 7.80 m on the east. It stands out from the castle walls 1.20 m on the north and 3.30 m on the east. The walls of tower IV are thicker than those of tower III as it is more exposed to attack. The north wall facing the channel is 1.20 m wide while the east wall, being more protected measures only 1 m across. Tower IV is badly preserved and it is difficult to record any other architectural information.

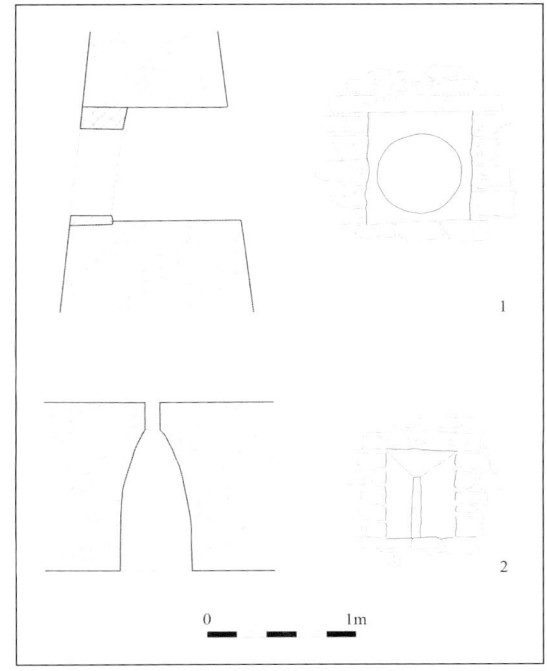

Fig 39 Ali Pasha's Castle, plans and elevations of a porthole and firing loop in the south wall

The entrances and internal structures

The castle has two gates, one in the middle of the east wall and a smaller second in the centre of the north wall. The east gate, Gate I, is 1.60 m wide on the outside broadening to 2.10 m on the inside. It stands up to 1.50 m high. The two parallel walls forming the entrance gateway are 1.60 m long and formerly supported a vaulted roof with a stone arch to the outside (the remains of which can still be seen).

Gate II in the north wall was later blocked. It was originally open to the Vivari Channel, as the castle wall on this side is set back only 1 m from the water. Being thus exposed, the gate was carefully protected. As well as towers guarding either side, the gate also possessed a fortified internal arrangement. Behind the north wall was a structure with three perpendicular chambers, each with a vaulted roof. The central chamber, 7.70 m long and 3 m wide, was a tunnel accessed via the gate and entirely open to the castle interior. The flanking chambers were accessed from the castle interior only through doorways. The one to the west measures 3.25 m wide and that to the east is narrower at 2.70 m wide.

The chamber on the east side was unlit and probably served as a gunpowder magazine, while the western chamber was equipped with firing loops covering the gate to the channel. Three of the loops are cut through the north castle wall, two facing towards the sea approach and the third directed at the immediate exterior of the gate. Another three firing loops opened through the chamber's east wall, 0.70 m thick, covering the interior gateway tunnel. Typically the firing loops are 0.70 m wide on the inside, narrowing to slits just 50-70 mm wide on the outside.

In addition to the parapet level walkway a second, lower stone platform runs along the inside of the castle on the west and south sides. To the west it is 1.40 m high and to the south 2 m high. It is difficult to interpret the function of this structure but it may simply have acted as an intermediate level between the low level of the castle interior and the parapet wall-walk. The remains of steps descending into the lower central area survive on the west while on the south side there are steps up to tower III.

The construction phases and dating

There are without doubt two construction phases to the castle, although it is difficult to define the character and original form of the castle without conducting archaeological excavations around the walls. The key to phasing the castle is in the northeast tower IV, which displays two separate building styles that can be reconciled elsewhere in the castle.

The north wall of the castle belongs to the first phase of construction and continues to form the inner western face of tower IV at a consistent width of 0.50 m. Subsequently, a batter measuring 0.70 m wide at its base was added to the north wall. This addition blocked the north gate and continues uninterrupted around the outer perimeter of tower IV.

The east wall of the castle is vertical and is the same width as the original north wall. Moreover, it passes behind the southern wall of tower IV, without the two being joined, and continues inside the tower thereby showing that it belongs to the earlier period of construction. Beyond the fact that more than one construction event is evident, the relationship of the east wall to the other rectangular tower, tower III, is less clear. The upper storey of tower III was used as a guard room and lit by two windows. It appears that the battered face of the tower is built over the curtain wall, but elsewhere the two appear contemporary. A side entrance to the west chamber of the north gate complex was blocked by the later insertion of masonry between here and tower II.

In its initial form, the building was not sufficiently fortified to serve military purposes.[9] It had thin vertical walls, 0.50-0.60 m wide, and it most likely had four towers. There were two gates, one landwards in the east wall and another opening onto the channel that was protected by firing loops in the north wall. The well-constructed left hand side of the gate was revealed in a small excavation. The three chambers at the north entrance complex were covered with stone-built vaults; above the central and western chambers the remains of a rectangular structure survive which probably served as residential space covered by a tiled roof. The area to the east was covered by an inclined roof, evidenced by a waterspout emerging from the base of the wall.

The first phase of construction can not be dated terribly early because the firing loops protecting the north entrance complex are designed for firearms rather than projectiles. A possible date for this phase could be around the year 1700.

During the second phase of construction the characteristics of the castle were changed entirely. Its defensive capabilities were reinforced by the closure of the north entrance, it being most vulnerable to attack from the Vivari Channel. The thickening and battering of the walls and the construction or reworking for cannon of the two circular towers demonstrates most clearly that the new function of the castle was the protection of Butrint from seaborne assaults.

The architecture and arrangement of the Vivari Channel castle is typical of Ali Pasha's other fortified sites. Characteristic features include: its regular geometric plan; the use of small squared stones in the walls set in horizontal courses; walls and towers of equal height; external battered walls; stone borders adorning the tops of walls and towers; narrow wall-walks; large splayed cannon embrasures; parapets pierced by firing loops; the defended entrance complex, and the siting of garderobes within the castle walls. These elements are all encountered, either in conjunction with, or as individual features, in other of Ali Pasha's fortifications, such as at the castles of Paleokastra, Tepelena, Porto Palermo and Libohova.

A more precise date for Ali's construction works on this castle may be ascertained from piecing together various historical events. The removal of the French from Corfu in 1799 did not satisfy the Pasha's ambitions. Under agreement on 21st April 1800 between Russia and Turkey, the Ionian islands were declared autonomous states (under Russian protection), with the title of the Republic of the

---

9 Editor's note: the original structure beneath the fortifications added by Ali Pasha may be part of a towered house belonging to Corfiote land owners the Gonemis, who held by grant the land of Wrina as a feudal estate. The building certainly appears on a Venetian cadastral map of 1718 and was noted by both Pouqueville and Leake. It only came in to the hands of Ali Pasha after 1804.

Seven Islands, while the coastal cities, excluding Parga which remained under Russian control, passed to the Ottomans (Zamputi 1967: 459). Directly after the Battle of Austerlitz (1805), Ali Pasha took advantage of discord between the Ottomans and Russians to capture Preveza, Vonitsa and Butrint (Alcaini 1823: 113). He subsequently established a military station at the fortified Monastery of Shën Gjergj north of Ksamil from where to control the land route to Butrint (Leake 1835: 102). Until *c.* 1806, Ali's relations with the French remained amicable enough. Taking care not to damage his separate agreement of *c.* 1803 with the English, Ali manoeuvred closer to the French extracting a promise from Pouqueville, Napoleon's consul-general to Ali Pasha's court at Ioannina, that he would become governor of Corfu once the island was regained by France.

The French, however, were not true to their word. Following the Treaties of Tilsit (1807), when France regained Corfu, rather than handing it over to the Pasha, the island's new commander Cezar Bertjé captured Parga as well and demanded Butrint from Ali (Boppe 1914: 92). General Bertjé understood that Butrint, as well as Corfu, was the key to dominance in the Adriatic Sea (Alcaini 1823: 118). At this time Ali had only a small garrison at Butrint and if Bertjé had attacked quickly a force of 500 men would have been sufficient to capture the fortress (Alcaini 1823: 118). In February 1808, the French received the grant of Butrint from the Ottoman Sultan, and were prepared to station a garrison of 3,000 troops at the ancient city (Boppe 1914: 96). The moment was lost though, and the Pasha readied reinforcements. England was only too happy to supply weapons to Ali to assist their navy expel the French from the Ionian Islands. With Butrint secured, during the following years Ali Pasha embarked on a number of military campaigns to extend and strengthen his dominion: Himara, Berat and Vlora all fell to the Pasha. In 1811 he captured Delvina and from there took Gjirokastra and Kardhiq.

Within the context of events at Butrint there are two likely periods when the Vivari castle may have been fortified: from 1798 to the beginning of 1799, or the period from 1807 to the seizure of the Seven Islands by the English in 1810. The later period is the time when relations with the masters of Corfu were most tense. To judge from the hasty construction techniques in this castle in comparison to Ali's fortifications at Gjirokastra, Tepelena, Libohova and Porto Palermo, it is suggested that it was built within a short period, immediately after the cession of Corfu to France in 1807 and Napoleon's demand for Butrint. 1807-1808 is the optimum time for Ali to have strengthened his position on the Corfu Straits.

Conclusions

In summing up the main results of this study, of Butrint in general and of its defensive constructions in particular, a number of conclusions can be made. There is no evidence from either the material culture or from the fortifications that Butrint was founded by Greek colonists. Within the chronological typology established for the city's fortifications, if a Greek colony had been present at Butrint, then the small enclosure of the earliest walls fashioned from un-worked stones around the acropolis would have to relate to such an event. The evidence does not justify the interpretation. It seems improbable that colonists would settle in such close proximity to the large fortified prehistoric centres at Kalivo, Vagalat and Karalibej (Plate 3). In addition, the frequent attribution of other constructions in the city to Greek colonists is not supported by the absolute chronology of the constructional sequences and styles.

Mention of Butrint as a 'city' from the end of the 6th to the beginning of the 5th century BC should not be equated with the presence of a developed fortification system. Neither the size of Butrint, the construction techniques visible nor any monumental buildings can be used to define a 'city' here at such an early date. The earliest indicators of development and prosperity date from the time when Butrint was included in the kingdom of Epirus. The first truly developed defensive structure dates from this time, and it can not be discounted as the work of King Pyrrhus (318-272 BC).

The different episodes of defensive works at Butrint could be correlated with different threats up to the period of the Roman occupation, when Butrint was the centre of an independent *koinon* (league or union) (c. 157-100 BC). Some defensive constructions, built without the use of mortar, appear to belong to an earlier period but actually relate to Roman times from the second half of the 1st century BC to the beginning of the 1st century AD (e.g. the lower southern wall). The same applies to certain other sections that have similar characteristics on the outside, whilst on the inside they are mortar bonded (e.g. the southern wall of the acropolis).

Other sections of apparently early but mortared walls can be found in the extension from the acropolis down to the Lake Gate as well as in the wall linking the acropolis with the lower southern wall. Thus, in the Roman period, there is an almost complete reconstruction of the fortified system. This fact, not considered by previous authors, testifies that during the times of Caesar and Augustus Butrint's Roman colonists felt the need to protect themselves from local threats. The so-called *Pax Romana* of Augustus was simply an exercise in propaganda and did not relate to actual events. Here we have indisputable evidence to set against Ugolini's unsubstantiated conclusions. He would surely have been astonished by the fact that the Romans – absolute rulers not only of Butrint but of the entire region – would have need to restore the fortified system of Butrint. It also reverses the judgement of Mustilli, that directly after the *Pax Romana*, the city was extended to the Vivari Channel with no necessity for fortification walls.

Butrint was re-fortified again in the 6th century at the time of the barbarian invasions though the remains of this period are slight.[10] After the reconstructions undertaken in the 1st century AD only a few adjustments would have been adequate to equip the city against barbarian incursions. The fortification of the Dema Wall was of great importance at this time, as the principal threat lay from overland rather than by sea.

Butrint maintained its important role in the Mediterranean during the early Middle Ages not just as a fortress, but as a city, a fact confirmed by documented events and the evidence provided by its fortifications. The medieval walls enclose more space than those of any previous periods and comprise many construction phases, which demonstrate the continuing importance of the city throughout the medieval period.

To withstand the Bulgarian invasion of the early Middle Ages, a complete reconstruction of Butrint's existing walls was undertaken and new extensions were added. The fortifications of the 9th-10th centuries were better provisioned than those of the Roman and late Roman periods since they, together with the natural protection afforded by Lake Butrint and the Vivari Channel, enclosed completely the enlarged area of the city developed in the Roman period. The waterfront circuit, completed prior to the Norman invasions, was bolstered by the landward protection from the 9th-10th century walls with triangular towers. However, the

---

10 Editor's note: recent excavations by the Butrint Foundation indicate that the late antique fortifications of Butrint date to the final quarter of the 5th century.

older, low and weak walls were not sufficiently durable for the age and this helps explain how the Norman adventurer Robert Guiscard easily captured the city; his assault was directed against this side, the weakest point of the city's defensive system.

The most developed period of Butrint's fortifications was during the time of the Despotate of Epirus, a period when construction works were undertaken throughout Albania, such as at Berat, Durrës, etc. On its west side the city was provided with a second line of walls and with high towers inside the old enceinte; the walls following the channel-side were supplemented with rectangular towers. The wall linking the acropolis with the Lake Gate was reconstructed and the neck of land between the acropolis and the lake to the north was closed off with new walls. On the highest point of the hill, a castle with a keep was built as part of a scheme to better protect the north side of the city.

After this time Butrint's importance as a fortified centre gradually waned. The surrounding walls enclosed a contracting community and there were insufficient people to protect the city. Defence of the city was primarily confined to the castle keep. The area around Butrint became progressively less secure and the purpose of the latest defensive works, concentrated on the banks of the Vivari Channel, reflects the imperative of preserving and controlling the rich fisheries.

With the dissolution of the Venetian Republic at the end of the 18th century, Butrint briefly re-emerged as a strategic base for Ali Pasha of Tepelena, who built the castle at the mouth of the Vivari Channel. However, even this late flourish did not last long. Butrint became thickly forested, serving only as a hunting ground for wild game. Only after more than a century had passed, during the period of the new national government in Albania, was Butrint re-born as an important cultural monument.

References

AA.VV. (1962) *Burime te zgjedhura per Historine e Shqiperise*, vol.2. Tirana, Instituti i Historisë dhe i Gjuhësisë.

AA.VV. (1998) *Albania: immagini e documenti dalla Biblioteca Nazionale Marciana e dalle collezioni del Museo Correr di Venezia*. Tirana, Istituto italiano di cultura.

Alcaini, C. (1823) *Biographie des Wesirs, Ali Pascha von Janina*. Vienna, n.n.

Anamali, S. (1981) Kontribut per historine e Buthrotit. In *Almanak, Saranda* 1: 16-24.

Baçe, A. (1971) Qyteti i fortifikuar i Beratit. *Monumentet* 2: 43-60.

Baçe, A. (1974) Qyteti i fortifikuar i Kanines. *Monumentet* 7-8: 25-55.

Baçe, A. (1979) Vështrim mbi arkitekturën e fortifikimeve antike në vendin tonë, *Monumentet* 17: 5-47.

Baçe, A. (1980) Banjat e shekujve të parë të e.r. në vendin tone. *Monumentet*19: 51-88.

Barone, N. (1887) *Notizie storiche tratte dai registri di cancelleria di re Carlo III di Durazzo*. Naples, Morano.

Becattini, F. (1788) *Storia ragionata dei Turchi, e degl'imperatori di Costantinopoli, di Germania, e di Russia, e d'altre potenze cristiane*. Venice, Pitteri and Sansoni.

Bellaire, J.P. (1805) *Précis des opérations générales de la division française de Levant*. Paris, n.n.

Beschi, L. (1968) La fortezza ellenica di Gyphtokastro. In *Les fortifications depuis l'antiquité jusqu'au Moyen-Age dans le monde mediterranéen*: 127-45. Athens, Technikon epimeleterion tes Ellados.

Boppe, A. (1914) *L'Albanie et Napoleon (1797-1814)*. Paris, Hachette.

Bozhori, K. and Budina, D. (1966) Disa mbishkjrime të pabotuara të teatrit të Butrintit. *Studime Historike* 1996.2: 143-91.

Budina, D. (1959) Nekropoli i Butrintit. . *Buletin i Universitetit Shtetëror të Tiranës (Seria e Shkencave Shoqërore* 2) 13: 246-56.

Budina, D. (1967) Ujësjellësi i Butrintit. *Studime Historike* 2: 145-51.

Budina, D. (1972) Antigonea. *Iliria* 2: 245-351.

Cabanes, P. (1974) Les inscriptions du theatre de Bouthrôtos. In, *Actes du colloque 1972 sur l'esclavage (Annales Littéraires de Besançon* 163): 105-209. Paris, Belles Lettres.

Cabanes, P. (1976) *L'Epire de la mort de Pyrrhos à la conquête romaine (272-167 av. J.C.)*. Paris, Belles Lettres.

Cabanes, P. (1981) Shoqeria dhe institucionet ne Epir dhe Maqedoni ne epoken klasike dhe helenistike. Iliria 11: 55-94.

Ceka, H. (1965) *Probleme te numismatikes ilire*. Tirane, Universiteti Shtetëror i Tiranes.

Ceka, H. (1967) Disa verejtje mbi mbishkrimet e pabotuara te teatrit te Butrintt. *Studime Historike* 1967.3 : 243-346.

Ceka, N. (1974) Fortifikime te vona antike prane Rruges Egnatia. *Monumentet* 7-8: 72-80.

Ceka, N. (1976) Fortifikimi antik i Butrintit dhe i territorit te Prasaibeve. *Monumentet* 12: 27-48.

Ceka, N. (1976) Fortifikimi antik i Butrintit. *Monumentet* 12: 27-48.

Çondi, D. (1981) Kontribut per harten arkeologjike te rrethit, ne Sarande. *Almanak, Saranda* 1: 12-16.

Cuntz, O. (ed.) (1990) *Itineraria Antonini Augusti et Burdigalense*. Stuttgart, B.G. Teubneri.

Dakaris, S. (1964) *Oi geneaologikoi-mytoi ton Moloson*. Athens, n.n.

Daux, G. (1949) Inscriptions de Delphes inédites ou revue. *Bulletin de Correspondance Hellenique* 73: 248-93.

Deroko, A. (1971) *Srednovekovni grad Skopje*. Belgrade, Srpska akademuja navka i umetnosti.

Drini, F. (1943) Luani i Butrintit. *Viti* 4.2 : 15-16.

Ducellier, A. (1981) *La façade maritime de l'Albanie au moyen age. Durazzo et Valona du XIe au XVe siècle*. Thessaloniki, Institute for Balkan Studies.

Faber, A. (1976) Contribution a la chronologie des fortifications dans l'Illyricum littoral. In M. Suic (ed.), *Jadranska obala u Protohistoriji: kulturni i etnicki problemi*: 227-46. Zagreb, Liber.

Franke, P.R. (1961) *Die antiken Munzen von Epirus*. Wiesbaden, Frank Steiner.

Geographus Ravennas (1929-40) *Itineraria romana*. Leipzig, B.G. Teubner.

Gratiani, I. (1728) *Historiarum Venetarum*. Patavii, Joannem Manfre.

Gregoire, H and de Keyser, R. (1939) *La chanson de Roland et Byzance, ou de l'utilité; du grec pour les romanistes*. Byzantion 14: 265-315.

Guarducci, M. (1953) Rassegna degli studi e della scoperte di inscrizioni preche in Italia, Creta, e Albania. In *Actes du deuxième Congrès International d'Èpigraphie Grecques et Latin*: 55-57. Paris, Maisonneuve.

Hammond, N.G.L. (1967) *Epirus*. Oxford, Clarendon Press.

Heuzey, L. and Daumet, H. (1876) *Mission Archeologique de Macedoine*. Paris, Librairie de Firmin-Didot.

References

Hopf, K. (1870) *Geschichte Griechenlands vom Beginn des Mittelalters bis auf unsere Zeit* (2 vols.). Leipzig, n.n.

Hrabak, B. (1970) Eksportimi i dritherave nga Shqiperia ne shekujt XIII, XIV, dhe XV. *Gjurmime Albanologjike* 1-2: 23-90.

Isambert, E. (1873) *Itineraire descriptif historique et archeologique de l'Orient.* Paris, Hachette.

Islami, S. (1975) Problemes de chronologie de la cite Illyrienne. In Utverdjena Ilirska Naselja. Posebna izdanja knjiga XXIV / *Coloques Internationales "Agglomerations fortifies Illyriennes"*: 37-45. Mostar, n.n.

Krumbacher, K. (1897) *Geschichte der byzantinischen Litteratur von Justinian bis zum Ende des oströmischen Reiches (527-1453)* (2nd ed.). Munich, C.H. Beck.

Lako, K. (1977-78) Gërmime në Butrint. *Iliria* 7-8: 293-99.

Lako, K. (1981a) Disa konkluzione paraprake mbi germimet arkeologjike ne Butrint (1975-1976). *Almanak, Saranda* 1: 23-39.

Lako, K. (1981b) Rezultatet e germimeve arkeologjike ne Butrint ne vitet 1975-76. *Iliria* 1: 93-154.

Leake, W.M. (1835) *Travels in Northern Greece* vol. 1. London, J. Rodwell.

Lugli, G. (1957) *La tecnica edilizia romana con particolare riguardo a Roma e Lazio* (2 vols). Rome, Bardi editore.

Luka, K. (1967) Toponimia shqiptare ne Kengen e Rolandit lidhur me disa ngjarje te viteve 1081-1085. *Studime Historike* 2: 127-44.

Marinesco, C. (1923) Alphonse V, roi d'Aragon et de Naples et l'Albanie de Scanderbeg. *Mélanges de l'École roumaine en France*: 1-185.

Marmora, A. (1672) *Della Historia di Corfu*. Venice, Curti.

Meksi, A. (1972) Arkitektura e kishës së Mesopotamit. *Monumentet* 3: 47-94.

Meksi, A. (1973) Arkitektura dhe restaurimi i kishes se Perondise. *Monumentet* 5-6: 19-42.

Meksi, A. (1975a) Disa kapela bizantine te vendit tone. *Monumentet* 10: 75-98.

Meksi, A. (1975b) Të dhëna të reja për kishën e Mesopotamit. *Monumentet*, 10: 151-60.

Meksi, A. (1976) Bazilika e madhe e Butrintit. *Mjeshtrit dhe arkitektura popullore*: 49-52. Tirana, 8 Nentori.

Meksi, A. (1977) Dy bazilika mesjetare të panjohura. *Monumentet* 13: 71-84.

Meyer, W. (1968) Entwicklung der Burgen in Deutschland, versuch einer Typologie. In *Les fortifications depuis l'antiquité jusqu'au Moyen-Age dans le monde méditerranéen (Actes VIII, Réunion Scientifique)*: 169-78. Athens, n.n.

Miller, K. (1988) Itineraria romana: römische Reisewege an der Hand der Tabula Peutingeriana. Bregenz , G. Husslein.

Miller, W. (1908) *Latins in the Levant*. London, J. Murray.
Monti, G.M. (n.d.) Corfu e le altre isole Ioniche. *Rassegna italiana* 54, fasc. 201.26.
Morosini, P. (1687) *Historia della citta e Republica di Venetia*. Venice, n.n.
Müller, C. and Müller T. (eds) (1841) *Fragmenta Historicorum Graecorum* vol. 1. Paris, n.n.
Mustilli, D. (1940) Gli scavi italiani di Butrinto. *Romana* 4: 183-91.
Mustilli, D. (1941) Relazione preliminare sugli scavi archeologici in Albania (1937-1940). *Atti della Reale Accademia d'Italia* 2: 677-704.
Nallbani, H. (1979) Mozaiku i baptisterit të Butrintit: ndërtim i njëkohëshëm. *Monumentet* 18: 57-64.
Nani, B. (1679) *Historia della Republica Veneta*. Venice, Combi e La Noù.
Nicol, D.M. (1957) *The Despotate of Epiros*. Oxford, Blackwell.
Nilsson M.P. (1909) *Studien zur Geschichte des alten Epeiros*. Lund, H. Ohlssons Buchdr.
Nilsson, M.P. (1951) *Cults, Myths, Oracles and Politics in Ancient Greece*. Lund, C.W.K. Gleerup.
Pani, G. (1976) Restaurimi i Portës me kulla në Butrint. *Monumentet* 11: 35-42.
Pouqueville, F.C.H.L. (1820) *Voyage dans la Grèce*. Paris, n.n.
Prendi, F. (1959) *Butrinti*. Tirana, Ministria i Arsimit dhe Kulturës.
Prendi, F. and Zheku, K. (1971) Qyteti ilir i Lisit. Origjina dhe sistemi i fortifikimit te tij. *Studime Historike* 1: 155-205.
Prendi, F. and Zheku, K. (1972) Lisi ne driten e te dhenave te reja arkeologjike. *Monumentet* 2: 7-21.
Remerand, G. (1928) *Ali de Tébélen, Pacha de Janina (1744-1822)*. Paris, Geuthner.
Rossi Taibbi, G. (1962) *Vita di sant' Elia il Giovane*. Palermo, Istituto siciliano di studi bizantini e neoellenici.
Sathas, K.N. (1882) *Dokumentes inédits relatifs à l'histoire de la Grèce au moyen âge*. Paris, Maisonneuve et Cie.
Scranton, R.L. (1941) *Greek Walls*. Cambridge, Mass., Harvard University Press.
Sestieri, P.C. (1942) Esplorazioni archeologiche in Albania 1941-42. *Rivista d'Albania* 3.3: 151-62.
Sestieri, P.C. (1943) Butrinti. *Viti* 4.4: 11-17.
Sestieri, P.C. (1959) Butrino. In *Enciclopedia dell'arte antica, classica e orientale* vol. 2: 232-35. Rome, Istituto della Enciclopedia Italiana.
Spahiu, H. and Komata, D. (1974) Shurdhahu-Sarda, qytet i fortifikuar mesjetar shqiptar. *Iliria* 3: 257-328.
Thalloczy, L., Jiricek, K. and Sufflay, M. (1913-1918) *Acta et Diplomatares Albaniae mediae aetatis illustrata*, 2 vols. Vienna, n.n.

Toy, S. (1955) *A History of Fortification from 3000 BC to AD 1700*. London, Heinemann.

Ugolini, L.M. (1927) *Ricerche archeologiche*. (*Albania antica* I). Rome/Milan, Società editrice d'arte illustrata.

Ugolini, L.M. (1934) Il batistero di Butrinto. *Revista di Archeologia Cristiana* 11: 265-83.

Ugolini, L.M. (1935) Il teatro di Butrinto. *Atti della Pontificia Accademia Romana di Archeologia, Rendiconti* 11.1-2: 81-94.

Ugolini, L.M. (1936) Il cristianesimo e l'organizzazione ecclesiastica a Butrinto. *Orientalia Christiana Periodica* 2: 309-29.

Ugolini, L.M. (1937) *Il mito d'Enea, Gli scavi*. Rome, Istituto Grafico Tiberino.

Ugolini, L.M. (1942) *L'Acropoli di Butrinto* (*Albania antica* III). Rome/Milan, Scalia.

Valentini, J. (1967-1975) *Acta Albaniae Veneta Saeculorum XIV et XV*. Munich/Palermo, n.n.

Vokotopullo, P. (1975) *I Ekklesiastiki Architektoniki eis tin dhitikin sterean Elladha kai tin Ipeiron-apo ton tellous ton 7 mehri ton lo 10 aionos*. Thesaloniki, n.n.

Winter, F.E. (1971) *Greek fortifications*. Toronto, University of Toronto Press.

Wrede, W. (1933) *Attische Mauern*. Athens, Deutsches Archäologisches Institut.

Zamputi, I. (1960) Disa flete te historise se Shqiperise ne periudhen 1506-1574. *Buletin i Universitetit Shtetëror të Tiranës* (*Seria e Shkencave Shoqërore* 2) 14: 3-31.

Zamputi, I. (ed.) (1967) *Dokumente te shek.XV për historinë e Shqipërisë 1479-1506*. Tirana, n.n.

Zamputi, I. (ed.) (1979) *Dokumente për historinë e Shqipërisë*. Tirana, n.n

Zheku, K. (1971) Restaurimi i Portë së Luanit, Butrint. *Monumentet* 1: 79-86.

Zheku, K. (1974) Restaurimi i portes se brendshme ne qytetin ilir te Lisit. *Monumentet* 7-8: 7-24.

Colour Plates

Plate 1 The location of Butrint in the Mediterranean

Plate 2 The Theatre

Plate 3 The regional location of Butrint showing fortified sites mentioned in the text

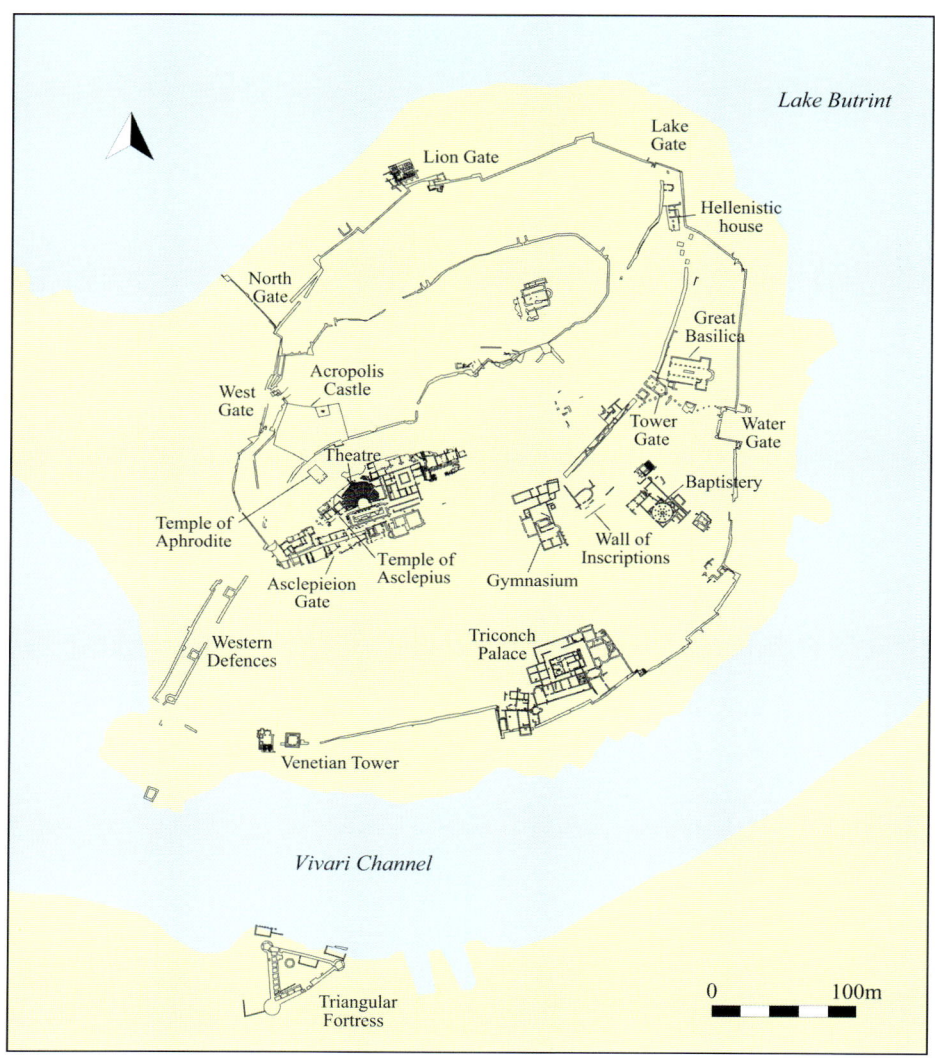

Plate 4 Butrint, monuments mentioned in the text

Colour Plates

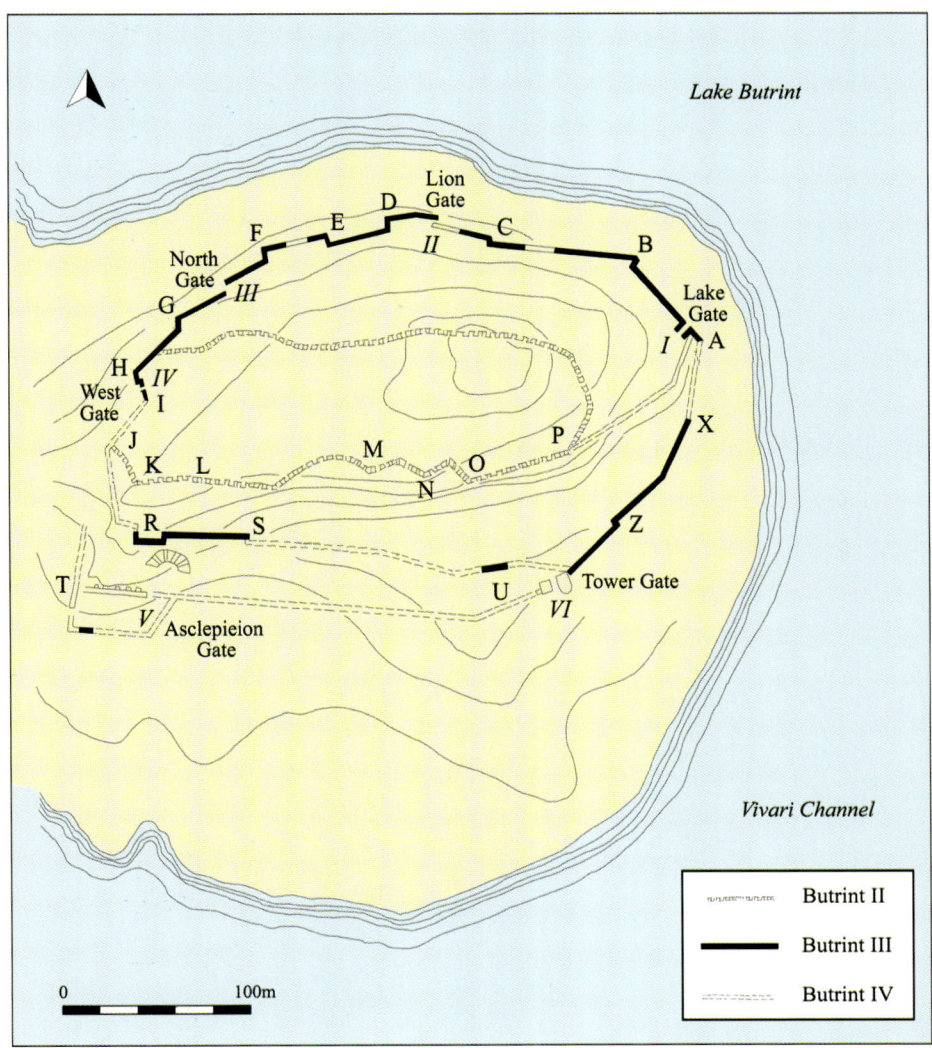

Plate 5 Construction sequence of ancient fortification walls at Butrint (after N. Ceka)

Plate 6 Prehistoric wall on south side of acropolis: un-worked blocks without mortar

Plate 7 Prehistoric wall on south side of acropolis: un-worked blocks without mortar

Plate 8 Prehistoric wall on south side of acropolis: detail of un-worked blocks without mortar

Colour Plates

Plate 9 Polygonal masonry on south side of acropolis

Plate 10 Polygonal masonry above the Theatre *analemma*

Plate 11 Polygonal and quadrangular masonry west of the Theatre

Plate 12 Polygonal masonry west of the Theatre

Plate 13 Coursed trapezoidal masonry on north side of the lower wall circuit

Plate 14 The Lake Gate

Colour Plates

Plate 15 The Lake Gate: detail of stone consoles

Plate 16 The Lake Gate, concealed entrance

Plate 17 The Lion Gate

Plate 18 The Lion Gate, interior

Plate 19 City wall adjacent to the Lion Gate

Plate 20 The Lion Gate, north interior wall

Plate 21 Re-built city wall between the Lake Gate and Lion Gate

Plate 22 The West Gate, north side

Colour Plates 143

Plate 23 Wall with pilasters south of the Theatre showing arched Asclepieion Gate to the rear

Plate 24 Wall with pilasters south of the Theatre

Plate 25 Wall with pilasters south of the Theatre

Plate 26 Wall with pilasters south of the Theatre

Plate 27 Polygonal wall with pilasters above Theatre analemma

Plate 28 Wall with pilasters south of the Theatre

Plate 29 The Tower Gate, U-shaped tower

Plate 30 The Tower Gate, pilaster in semicircular section of U-shaped tower

Plate 31 The Tower Gate, pilaster in square section of U-shaped tower

Plate 32 Wall northeast of the Tower Gate

Plate 33 The Baptistery

Plate 34 The Baptistery, detail of mosaic pavement

Colour Plates 149

Plate 35 The Great Basilica

Plate 36 The Dema Wall (Instituti i Arkeologjisë)

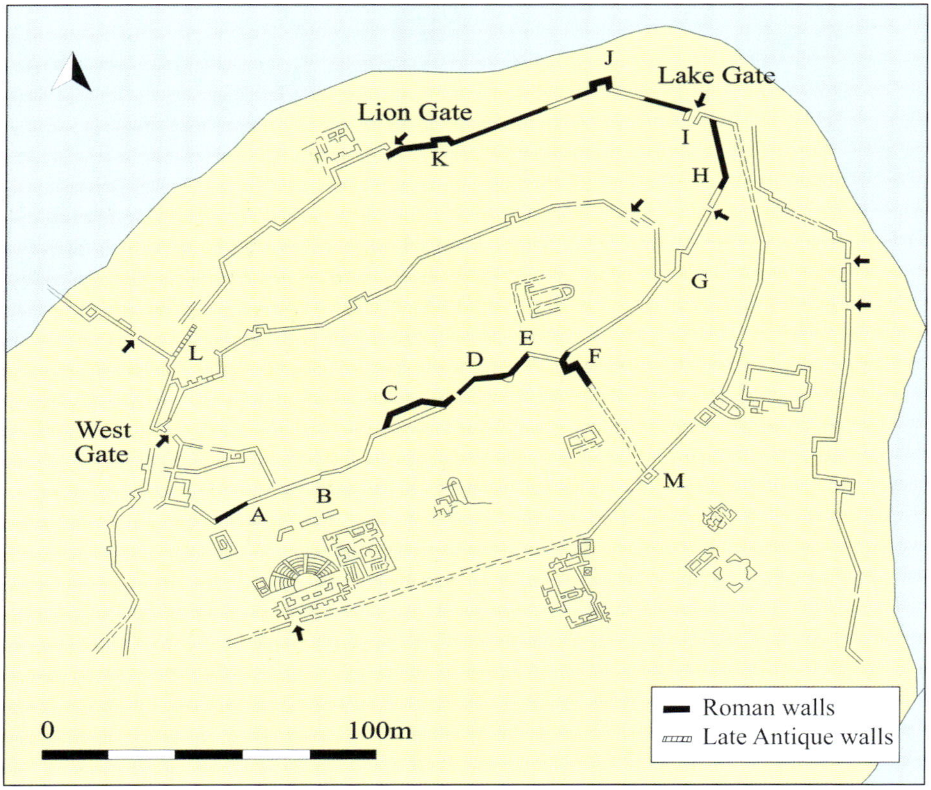

Plate 37 Fortifications at Butrint dated to between the 1st century BC and the 6th century AD

Plate 38 Opus quadratum in wall section H-I (cf. Plate 37)

Colour Plates   151

Plate 39 Roman stylistic building device: scored mortar

Plate 40 Opus reticulatum in wall between the Lake Gate and Lion Gate

Plate 41 The Tower of Inscriptions (Instituti i Arkeologjisë)

Plate 42 The Wall of Inscriptions

Colour Plates

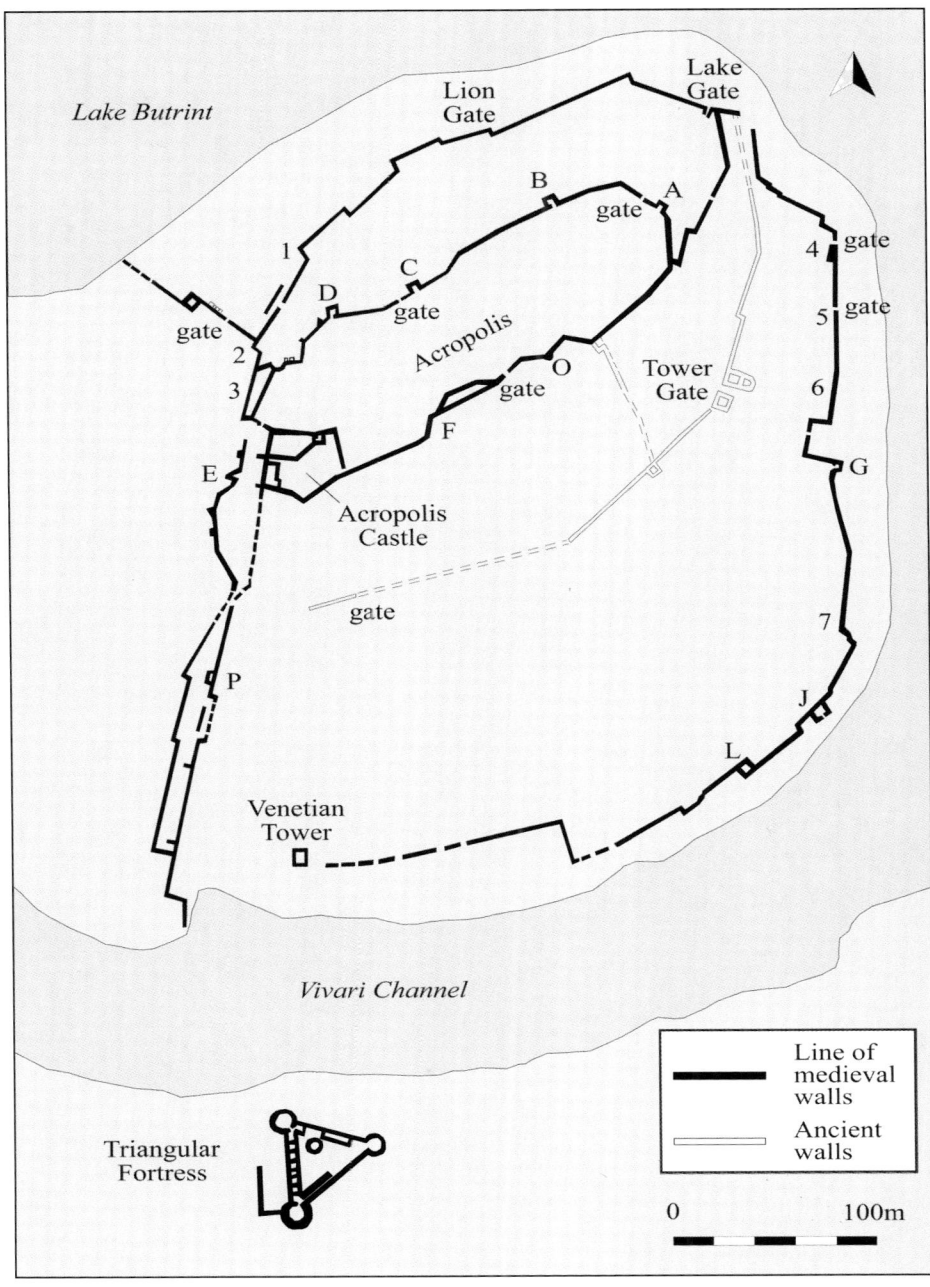

Plate 43 Medieval fortifications at Butrint

Plate 44 Guard room (cf. Plate 43 point 3)

Plate 45 Guard room garderobe and firing loop

Plate 46 Guard room firing loop

Plate 47 Remains of a pilaster on the wall southwest of tower E

Plate 48 Tower E, north-facing elevation

Plate 49 Tower L, south-facing elevation

Plate 50 Tower L, firing loops

Plate 51 City wall and tower J

Plate 52 City wall between towers G and J

Plate 53 Tower G, south-facing elevation

Colour Plates

Plate 54 Tower G, firing loop

Plate 55 Tower G, west-facing elevation showing doorways

Plate 56 The Water Gate, interior elevation

Plate 57 The Water Gate entrance, exterior view

Colour Plates

Plate 58 The 'closing' wall linking the acropolis to Lake Butrint

Plate 59 Construction phase 1 in the 'closing' wall linking the acropolis to Lake Butrint (south side)

Plate 60 Tower on the 'closing' wall (northwest side)

Plate 61 Various construction phases in the 'closing' wall linking the acropolis to Lake Butrint (north side showing battlements and wall-walk)

Colour Plates

Plate 62 Phase 1 acropolis wall circuit west of tower D

Plate 63 Phase 2 acropolis wall circuit between towers C and B

Plate 64 Square putlog wall construction on north side of acropolis wall circuit

Plate 65 Tower B, east-facing elevation

Plate 66 Door in the southern acropolis wall

Plate 67 Tower O, northeast-facing elevation

Plate 68 The castle and 'closing' wall

Plate 69 The reconstructed castle keep and battlements on the east enclosure wall

Colour Plates

Plate 70 Reconstructed wall-walk and cannon ports on east side of castle enclosure

Plate 71 Cannon in reconstructed castle cannon port

Plate 72 The Triangular Fortress and Venetian Tower from the Acropolis Castle

Plate 73 The Triangular Fortress, phase 1 firing loop blocked by construction of tower I

Colour Plates

Plate 74 The Triangular Fortress, southwest elevation of tower I

Plate 75 The Triangular Fortress, phase 1 firing loop made redundant by building of tower III

Plate 76 The Triangular Fortress, wall-walk and firing loops on north wall

Plate 77 The Triangular Fortress, phase 1 firing loop

Plate 78 The Triangular Fortress, north wall wall-walk and internal structure

Plate 79 The Triangular Fortress, south gate

Plate 80 The Triangular Fortress, tower I upper storey windows

Plate 81 The Triangular Fortress, northwest-facing elevation of tower II

Plate 82 The Triangular Fortress, late Venetian doorway

Plate 83 The Triangular Fortress, east-facing elevation of tower III

Plate 84 The Triangular Fortress, carving of the Lion of St Mark in arch above late Venetian doorway

Plate 85 The Triangular Fortress, circular gunpowder magazine

Plate 86 The Venetian Tower, south-facing elevation

Plate 87 The Watchtower and Vivari Channel

Plate 88 The Watchtower, north-facing elevation

Colour Plates

Plate 89 Ali Pasha's Castle, from the Vivari Channel

Plate 90 Ali Pasha's Castle, east-facing elevation of tower III

Plate 91 Ali Pasha's Castle, porthole in the south wall